Speak Your Horse's Language:
Communicating with the Driving Horse

By: Gloria Austin
President of:
Equine Heritage Institute, Inc. (EHI)

ISBN: 978-1-7320805-0-8
First Publish Date 2018

Copyright © 2018 by Equine Heritage Institute, Inc.

All rights reserved. No part of this publication may be reproduced, distributed, or transmitted in any form or by any means, including photocopying, recording, or other electronic or mechanical methods, without the prior written permission of the publisher, except in the case of brief quotations embodied in critical reviews and certain other noncommercial uses permitted by copyright law. For permission requests, write to the publisher, addressed "Attention: Permissions Coordinator," at the address below.

Gloria Austin Carriage Collection, LLC; Equine Heritage Institute, Inc.
3024 Marion County Road Weirsdale, FL 32195 Office: (352) 753-2826 Fax: (352) 753-6186

Ordering Information:
Quantity sales: Special discounts are available on quantity purchases by corporations, associations, and others. For details, contact the publisher at the address above.
Printed in the United States of America
First Edition

Table of Contents

FORWARD ... 4

HOW I LEARNED TO LISTEN TO HORSES ... 5

BOOKS I HAVE WRITTEN ... 30

UNDERSTANDING THE HORSE'S MIND & BEHAVIOR ... 32

CHOOSING A HORSE ... 58

TALKING WITH A HORSE ... 84

TRANSLATING RIDING TO DRIVING ... 105

TALKING WITH TACK ... 127

DRIVING STYLES ... 143

THE HARNESS ... 151

THE CARRIAGE ... 158

TYPE OF CARRIAGE ... 161

PLACES TO TRAIN ... 166

LEARN YOUR TRAFFIC SIGNALS AND SALUTES ... 177

SAFETY ... 178

MOST COMMON PROBLEMS ... 179

PROBLEMS ... 184

EDUCATE YOURSELF ... 196

Forward

In the 50's, I listened to 'Francis the Talking Mule' engage in dialogue with Donald O'Connor. In the 60's, Wilbur talked to 'Mr. Ed' in the CBS special series starring a palomino American Saddlebred. In the 80's and 90's we heard horse trainers talk about "round pen reasoning." How do the average horsemen and women communicate with horses? What are the factors that even make it possible? You will learn the underpinning of horsemanship, which is based on bonding to create trust and then communication to get the behavior you want in your driving horse.

Often in history, the talent of communicating with horses was kept a secret. In the past, the expression "horse whisperer" came from the notion that the trainer or communicator was thought to whisper something magical in the horse's ear to make it behave and perform. Many of the trade societies have held their skills a secret. Today, "Natural Horsemanship" is the label for shared systems of training horses derived from observing free-roaming horses and using those techniques they use with one another to direct our horses of today.

Even though this book will reveal some of my secrets as they pertain to the driving horse, the rider can also learn from reading this book. I will touch on riding to elaborate on some similarities and differences, but remember our focus is the magic of talking to driving horses. The first part of the book tells of my personal history with horses and the people that were instrumental in my life. The second part will tell about the elements of bonding with the horse, and the third will talk about the aids for communication and how to use them.

Keep in mind that each horse or pony is different with individual personalities and varying experiences. Each horse owner or handler is different with individual personalities and varying experiences. Therefore, there are no hard and fast rules governing these relationships. It should also be noted that the timing and act of communication can be influenced by each encounter under a variety of circumstances which are almost impossible to predict so human judgment must be developed through experience and there is no substitute for experience. You must "do" to learn about behavior, relationships, and communication. So have fun and do. Learn and become wise.

Safety will also be mentioned, and we all must remember that each person who works with horses may have different approaches. My 35 years of experience with horses from all over the world has given me insights which should be helpful. Especially to those of you who have enjoyed horses, but now find it "Time to Drive."

HOW I LEARNED TO LISTEN TO HORSES

Always Listening!

What an Influence!

My interest in the history of the horse came in the 1980's from reading Harold B. Barclay's book, "The Role of the Horse in Man's Culture." As a horseman himself, Barkley's admiration for the role of the horse throughout the ages gave him an understanding of the horse's influence when ridden or driven two-wheeled vehicles.

Barkley covers the origins of the domesticated horse in relationship to other animals. He also writes about the spread of the horse culture from the vast grassy plains of Eurasia to the east, west, and south through the open expanse of what are now Asia, Europe, and Africa. He also traces man's use of the horse on to the Americas.

The feeling of power, mobility, and freedom that I feel through my relationship with the horse was experienced by many throughout history. Barkley had a sense of the personal significance of the horse.

The psychological aspect of this relationship and the practical application of the horse's power and speed led to the use of the horse for warfare, transportation, trade, commerce, agriculture, and industry.

Today the recreational use of horses and equine-assisted therapy programs take advantage of this sense of well-being through the touch and interaction with this strong and powerful animal. Equine-assisted education can be an easy way to interest students of all ages to study history, humanities, science and animal husbandry.

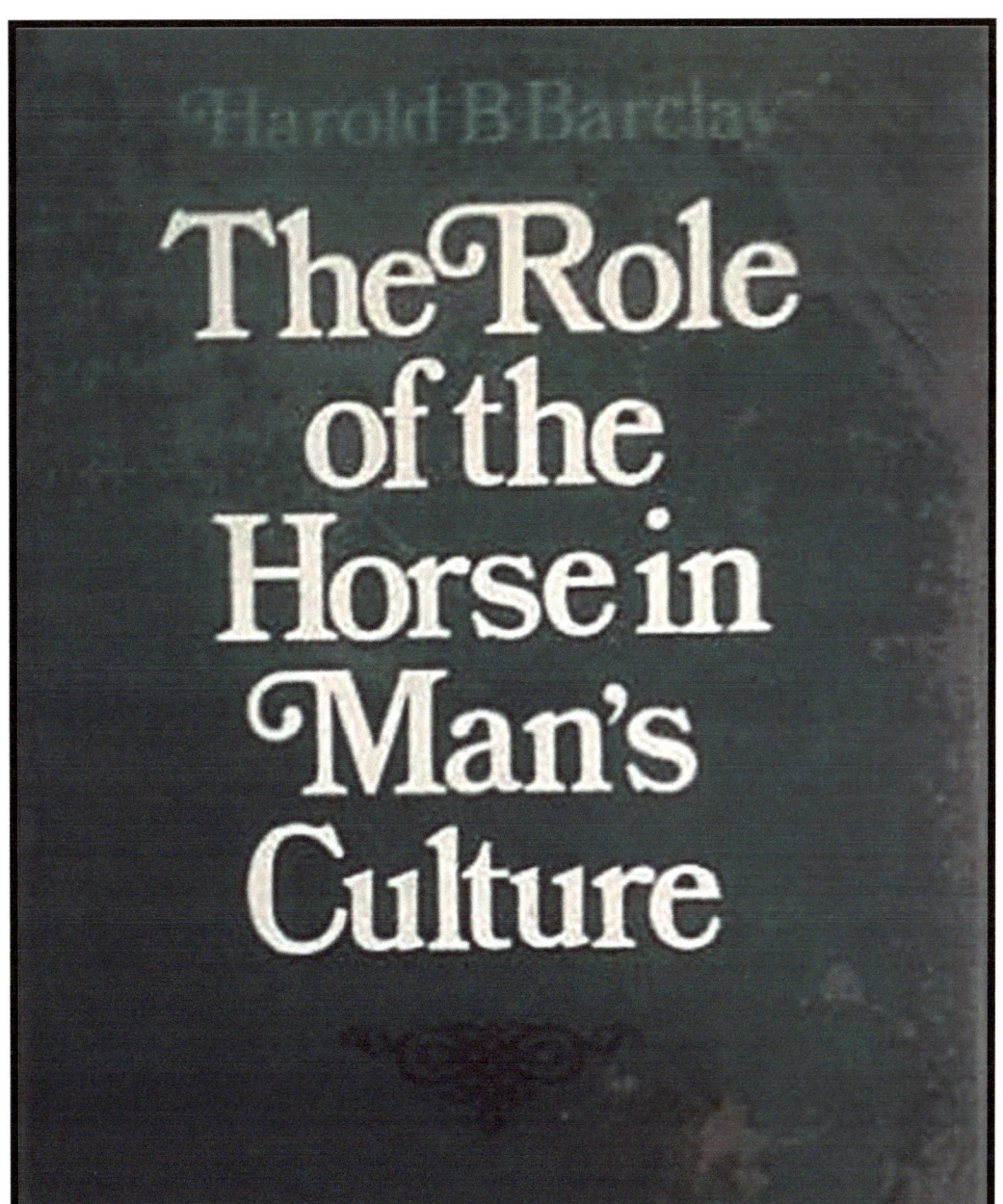

The Influence of Ancient Writings

Well before Barclay's book, the first people to have a horse training manual were the Hittites, the Indo-European horsemen. They introduced domesticated horses to Asia Minor, the Middle East, and Africa sometime between 1900-1800 BCE. These people used horses and chariots for hunting, warfare, and ceremonies.

This manual is the earliest known writing that talks about the care and training of horses. The author, Kikkuli, was the Hurrian, "master horse trainer," of the land known as Mitanni. It is a manual about chariot horse training and is written in the Hittite language, dating to the Hittite New Kingdom.

This writing dated about 1360 BCE, talks about the care and training of horses. Kikkuli describes 184 days of training in pairs. He outlines diet, watering, workouts and periods of rest. These Hittite horses were conditioned to travel up to sixty miles a day at different paces.

The Hittites defeated Ramses II at Kadesh in Syria, using 3500 chariots in the year 1286 BCE. The training must have worked!

Mounted cavalry began to replace chariot forces around 1000 BCE. These soldiers and warriors who fought on horseback also dismounted to fight from the ground. They were highly mobile warriors.

The ridden horse offered nomadic societies greater range to spread ideas and technology throughout the lands.

Around 350 BCE Xenophon, a Greek writer, wrote treatises on horsemanship. He wrote "The Duties of a Cavalry Commander" and "On the Art of Horsemanship." The modern horse person would enjoy referring to these texts to understand the similarities and differences in knowledge of horses today and that of our forerunners.

There are sections that describe the selection, care and training of horses. Xenophon also outlines the principles of classical dressage as well as the use of no-abrasive training methodologies.

In Xenophon's words: "A horse is a thing of beauty... none will tire of looking at him as long as he displays himself in his splendor."

He also is noted for saying, "For what the horse does under compulsion, as Simon also observes, is done without understanding; and there is no beauty in it either, any more than if one should whip and spur a dancer."

The ancient Greek horseman did not use a saddle and had no stirrups. He sat with his bare buttocks on the horse's back. The rider's legs hung down to grip the horse's side for balance and keeping a deep seat. Once the saddle and stirrups were developed, the rider had greater security and leverage for slashing swordsman and there was greater stability of the mounted archer as well.

When the horse arrived in the New World, The North American Plains Indians use of the horse offered greater mobility and range for travel and hunting. These Native Americans were exquisite bareback riders, just as the Greeks were generations before.

Often these classic writers have an offering for today's horse person since the horse is the same animal of yesterday as it is today. New riders are often taught to ride without the use of stirrups to improve their seat and leg strength. Knowledge of these very early people offered me an insight into the use of horses and their preparation for driving in today's culture. We naturally make far too little use of our modern horses.

The Influences of the Horse on the World

Forgive the puns, but the horse is one catalyst that transformed the world once its speed and power were "harnessed." It was the first thing that allowed man to travel faster than his two legs could carry him on land. The horse has been a part of warfare, commerce, industry, transportation, and agriculture throughout the centuries. It has the "horsepower" to do our work and travel more efficient. It is the creature that we, as equestrian enthusiasts, known as the "driving force" in our day-to-day lives. It is our joy and our recreation. It is our friend and companion. It is our means of expression to the world.

I am pictured to the right with my eldest granddaughter, Amy Lee Golisano driving a wicker Phaeton. In the picture below, I am with Gene Serra, MD, my life partner. He is sitting on the front gammon seat of my blue coach manufactured by Healey & Company.

6,000 Years of History with the Horse

I am often quoted as saying, "We have had over 6,000 years of history with the domesticated horse and only about one hundred years with the automobile." This understanding seems to put things in perspective. This statement helps to educate humanity and give appreciation to the horse for its transformative impact on man's culture. This companion of man has brought us the world as we know it today. Through prehistoric times, early civilizations, medieval times, the establishment of empires, the Renaissance, the Age of Discovery, and the settling of the New World - the horse has marched through history with its power and speed. I commonly use this timeline, below, but you will have to squint to see the small automobile in the lower right corner to see our brief time with self-propelled transportation.

Innovations made humanity's life easier. Inventions like rope to tether the horse, the slide car and sledge for dragging things behind the horse advanced culture. The wheel for its efficiencies, combined with the horse allowed the movement of cargo and people. The stirrup provided the rider stability when on the horse's back. The full collar gave the horse the ability to pull heavier loads and drag agricultural equipment. All these inventions and more, made man's work easier and lead to greater mobility and production.

Horses have been selectively bred for generations and today over 300 breeds exist in the world. There is still a myriad of uses for the horse primarily for recreation, therapy, and education. What I hope is that this book brings you a better understanding of yourself and your horse.

My Path of Discovery

My path of discovery started with my father who, as a farmer and cattle dealer, was using tractors on our 1,000 acres in upstate New York. Everyone needs a role model and a person that encourages their interests. My father was that to me.

He bought my first horse and gave me my first advice on communicating with the horse with instructions of no running or racing my horse near the stable. "You will walk your horse away from the barn and walk to the barn." Little did I understand how valuable this advice was at the time. I just knew I needed to obey if I wanted to keep riding my horse through the beautiful New York State Southern Tier countryside and gather cattle.

My father's first job after graduating from eighth grade was to drive a pair of draft horses on road construction in Steuben County. He is pictured in the upper right photo. He was too small to do manual labor, so he was assigned two draft horses to do the work on road construction. His experiences with horses served him well when it was time to do farming work with horses at my childhood farm.

I had six horses during my childhood; an American Saddlebred, a Hackney Pony, a Shetland Pony, a Palomino Quarter Horse, a black and white pinto, and a big white mare that must have been part Percheron.

Just as my first riding horses offered me an understanding of horses, these early childhood experiences set the stage for a lifetime of enjoyment and knowledge that I want to pass on to you in this book, "All Horses Talk - Communicating with the Driving Horse."

My Enjoyment of Riding

My childhood was spent gathering livestock on the farm and competing in gymkhana at the local horse shows. I am pictured here with Duke, my first saddle horse. I sold my last childhood horse to help pay for my college. I was moving into adulthood with all the typical responsibilities.

After 20 years raising a family, working in government planning, and the corporate world processing payroll for small companies, riding became my recreation. I could finally afford a saddle horse again, but quickly moved to driving as the rigors of the trot and canter on the back of a horse took its toll on my much older body.

Studying ridden dressage and quadrille with Major Carlos A. Mancero of Ecuador and Ocklawaha, Florida, I further refined my abilities to direct the footfalls of the horse. John Lyons, of natural horsemanship fame, also contributed to my skills at communicating with the saddle horse.

There was an interesting phenomenon - all of these horse whisperers were calm, confident and patient. They never angered. They never moved quickly and never exhibited aggression.

Riding to Driving

The joy of riding horses led me to a love of driving horses. In my adult years, I also took my hand to breeding and training driving horses and miniature horses. In my formative years of driving, I produced a training video with a companion booklet "Easy and Enjoyable, Driving Your Horse." Some basic principles of communication seem to persist and now are worth sharing with you in this book.

Communication is a two-way street, as most of us know, but the horse is a silent animal, so how do we get feedback? Without a spoken language, how do we send messages to the horse? Other factors become apparent in dialogue with these animals that are bigger and stronger than we are.

Horses also seem to sense our emotions and know if we are happy, sad, fearful, or excited.

Their size precludes them from being forced to do what we want, so good communication must be based on bonding, trust, and feedback. The message must be sent and received with understanding to achieve the correct behavioral response.

Learning About Driving

Driving at shows with restored traditional carriages at Walnut Hill Farm Driving Competition, East Aurora Driving Competition, and Lorenzo Driving Competition in Cazenovia in New York State consumed my early interest in driving. Local club activities, driving at the hunt races, picnic drives, and promenades gave me an opportunity to develop more driving skills.

Retired from a career in business, Earle Billington (pictured on the bottom left), was the stable manager of a small facility in Pittsford, NY where I boarded five horses. He offered me a first-hand understanding of driving. He had grown up driving horses on his childhood farm and gave me very practical advice. When I developed the Mendon Equestrian Center, a boarding, and breeding stable, Earle moved his horses there.

I studied pair driving with Hungarian Driving Master Leslie Kozsely. Dr. Leslie M. Kozsely (1922-2007) pictured below on the right, was one of my early carriage driving mentors. He established the American Four-In-Hand Training Center in Auburn, New York. Leslie's contribution to carriage driving in America was profound. He was a founding member of the American Driving Society and an early member of the Carriage Association of America, of which he was an honorary, lifetime director. His confidence and gentlemanly demeanor always impressed me.

Once in Florida, combined driving at Live Oak Competition and recreational driving in the Ocala National Forest offered me an even greater understanding of the maneuverability of the driving horse and carriages.

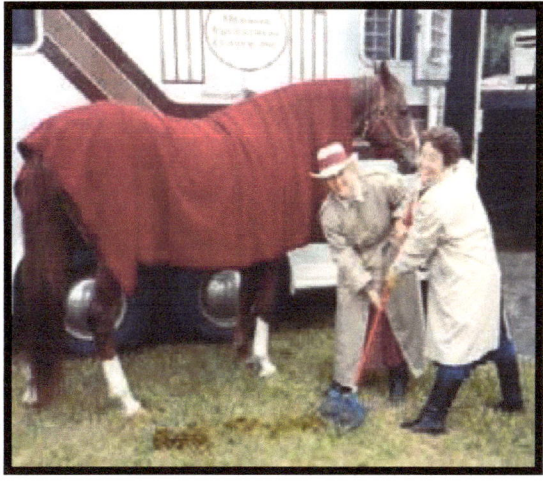

My Coachmen and Coachwoman

Jean-Paul Gautier, Coachman

Jean-Paul Gautier was educated and trained in carriage driving in France at the Institu Francais du Cheval. From Canada, Jean-Paul migrated to the USA and worked for me as a private coachman from 1998 to 2002. His expertise in horsemanship and driving horses and large trucks came in handy when I traveled to Europe with many horses and drove a four-in-hand on my European adventure to six countries. My travels also took me to Colorado. There, Jean-Paul is fondly remembered driving my reproduction Concord stagecoach. He and fellow Canadian Horn Sounder, Dale Romagnoli are pictured to the right. Jean-Paul was a master at dressing the part. Here you see him unshaven and serious-faced, which was seldom seen when off the stagecoach.

Even though Jean-Paul was trained in France, he was taught the English system of driving. For this Colorado occasion, he grabbed three reins in each hand to drive six of my dark Friesian horses. Melissa Warner can be seen on the outriding pinto horse below.

Melissa Warner, Coachwoman

After acting as an equine specialist for two years, Melissa became my private coachwoman for the next nine years and organized travels to Europe and all over the United States and Canada. Under Ms. Warner's leadership of our trained staff, we traveled to Belgium, The Netherlands, England, France, Germany, and Luxemburg where I successfully competed in driving events requiring classic carriages.

Melissa's background in showing American Saddlebreds under saddle seat equipped her to present one of my horses in the more traditional sidesaddle. Her posture and elegance allowed her to demonstrate my traditional carriages with grace. With my knowledge of classical turnout, we made a great team.

Her organizational skills allowed her to unravel the task of putting together a carnet for travel with horses abroad so that she and our grooms could travel on the same airplane as the horses. You could have tracked my trip by her calls to European feed stores for delivery of grain at our next destination. I felt like the logistics specialist coordinating people, horses, supplies, transport, events, and operations at various sites around Europe. Melissa's care of the horses and staff made my job much easier when traveling afar and at home in the USA and Canada.

David E. Saunders, Coachman

Contributing to my understanding of the horse is private coachman, David. E. Saunders. David has worked for me off and on over many years. I have shared many of my insights with David and, since he also worked for the Queen of England and was Prince Philip's private coachman for almost 20 years, we shared an interest in classical driving, and Full State turnouts like you see below with my Austrian Armbruster Dress Chariot.

He is pictured driving the "Austin Grays" (Pure Spanish Horses) to Cinderella's pumpkin carriage at Disney World in Orlando, Florida. At SECAB, a breed show in Seville, Spain, he presented the unique "Gloria's Diamond"–one horse in the wheel position, two horses in the swing position, and one horse in the lead. He also drove my Austrian Dress Chariot to six of my PRE horses for the Carriage Association of America's Learning Weekend in 2017.

Influential People in My Life

Patrick Schroven

Patrick Schroven has been restoring original carriages since 1975, using rational craftsmanship and authentic materials. His restoration shop is located in the heart of Europe and is noted for quality restoration of some of the finest carriages in the world. His familiarity with private carriage collections, the best museums, and Royal household collections, Patrick acquainted me with the living history of European carriages as we toured Western Europe.

Henk van der Wiel

It is through friendship with Belgium harness maker, Henk Van der Wiel that I became a member of the Private Driving Club of Europe. This group of people, with their club tours, is how I came to understand Eastern European culture and carriages. I have been blessed to participate, with my horses, in many of their horsed outings throughout Belgium, France, Germany, Luxemburg, and The Netherlands.

Gordon Wright

Gordon Wright was universally acclaimed as one of the most influential horsemen of his generation. I learned three major things years ago from, at the time, this 84-year-old teacher of riding:

- "Never look down."
- "It is the rider's fault."
- "The horse has to think that God is in its mouth and the devil is at its side."

From Driving Singles to Four-in-Hand

I have been driving what is called a "four-in-hand" for over 20 years, and before that, I drove singles and pairs of horses. I have competed in both modern and traditional driving events. Some may know of my miniature horse breeding farm and boarding stable, Mendon Equestrian Center, in Honeoye Falls, New York. Many used my video and booklet to train their miniature horses to drive.

I am currently a member of the Carriage Association of America, Carriage Museum of America, American Driving Society, World Coaching Club, United States Equestrian Federation, Four-in-hand Club, European Private Driving Club and the Four-in-hand Club of Philadelphia.

Four-in-hand driving means the driver (or "whip" as the person is called) holds four reins in the left hand and uses the right hand to hold the whip and manipulate the reins.

I call this system the "British Hand." It was further modified by the German Achenbach but is derived from the coachmen of England who used to drive four horses and large coaches full of mail, parcels, and passengers for great distances over a network of roads. When using this technique, the driver could rest his left hand on occasion by putting his right over the top of the left to hold the reins. This British technique also allows the driver to place the whip atop the reins of the left hand to operate the handbrake or shake hands. With the whip alone in the right hand, the driver can signal turns and stops.

Driving in Europe

After winning four-in-hand and coaching championships in the USA and Canada in 1998, I took horses, carriages, and staff to tour Europe, which included participating in an Attelage de Tradition, in Cuts, France in 1999. These competitions are one-day driving shows of antique carriages with 65 points deducted for using a new reproduction carriage.

The three phases of these events include Presentation at three stations, Routier over the course of about 15 miles, and Maniabilité, which is through as many as 20 sets of cones.

Started by Marque Christian and Marques Antoinette de Langlade, these events have become famous throughout Europe. Here I am seen driving my Guiet coach once owned by the Bugatti family. I drove this coach back in France one hundred years after it was manufactured in France in 1899. I am seen with Coachman Jean-Paul Gautier.

After this first adventure, annual travels to Europe to drive with the Private Driving Club and to compete in Attelage de Traditions became regular. I stabled at Henk Vander Weil's Stable and ventured throughout this continent to drive a variety of different breeds of horses and types of carriages.

All Around the World—"A Horse Is a Horse"

The Chateau de Cuts has seen many horses, carriages, and parties in its day. It's a chateau to the French and a palace or country house to the English, and it is the family home of the Marquis and Marques de Langlade's family who know how to throw a party. This one was sponsored by Pommery Champagne, with four wine glasses setting at each place. The world of carriage drivers seems to be a genteel world.

I learned that driving horses in France is just like driving horses in the USA or Canada or any other place in the world. A horse is a horse, here or there, and you communicate in much the same fashion, here or there. The French language may be different, but horses seem to respond to intonation as much as the words. The Dutch and Spanish horses became familiar with my voice and the English language rather quickly.

"How can we know the dancer from the dance?"

William Butler Yeats

I have been fortunate to have driven four-in-hands on four continents, in 15 countries, holding four reins of at least 17 different breeds/types of horses. To the right, I am seen driving four Andalusians put to a Hooper roof seat break in Cuts, France at an Attelage de Tradition. I have been fortunate to win many pleasure driving championships here in the USA and Canada over the years.

Even though my passion is driving and collecting carriages, I have ridden many breeds and even rode a comfortable ambling Paso Fino on trail rides up and down the East Coast of the United States for 19 years.

Interestingly, a similar upper body posture or frame used in driving is used in dancing. The core muscles of the human body have to be developed to sit erect on a carriage seat for an extended period. As the driver looks in the direction of the turn, the upper body rotates ever so slightly to direct the horse. It is much the same in dancing.

I am proud to be a championship ballroom dancer winning several titles with my life partner, Dr. Gene Serra. Dr. Serra is a retired general surgeon who is originally from the Philippines and has over 40 years of practicing medicine in Central Florida.

The posture and frame of the upper torso are much the same in dancing and driving. If the leader looks in the direction of the turn, it should cue the partner in dancing as well as the driving horse to do the same.

Learning About Carriages

Listening to lectures given by Kenneth Wheeling and others at the Carriage Association of America's Conferences gave me a keen awareness of the value and history of carriages.

My avid interest in books from the 1700's and 1800's, to compare contemporary knowledge of that of yesteryear, gave way to my own set of principles.

Travel throughout Europe opened my eyes to the history and the elegance of carriages. I visited carriage collections in museums and private stables of the royals of Europe. Austria, Germany, The Netherlands, Belgium, and France were favorite destinations traveling with horsemen, restorers, and collectors. These historical destinations were exciting and brought about a discerning eye.

Soon the lure of driving four horses to a large English style coach took hold after watching the gentlemen drive in the coaching classes at the Royal Winter Agricultural Fair in Toronto, Canada. The rest is history. Hungarian master horseman, Dr. Leslie Kozsely, and British coachman, David E. Saunders, both contributed to my ability to drive four and go on to encourage others to enjoy the pleasures of driving.

Sharing the experiences at Martin's Carriage Auctions allowed me to acquire an interest in antique and classic carriages.

The Carriage Association of America

The Carriage Association of America (CAA) was founded in 1960 and is the oldest and largest international organization devoted to the preservation and restoration of animal-drawn carriages and sleighs. They also sponsor driving events and shows, stressing the importance of restored, classical, and conserved antique carriages.

It is through this organization that I also shared the pleasures of collecting, driving, and learning more about carriages and driving. For more information, please go to www.carriageassociationofamerica.com.

The pictures at the right are of a restored Shanks Mail Phaeton being judged in 1999 in French Lick, Indiana at the Annual CAA conference where this restoration, by Patrick Schroven, won first place and the highest overall award at the conference.

With over 3,000 members from all over the world, this organization helps to preserve the culture and history of carriages.

Putting Together Unusual Turnouts

I have always taken an interest in turnouts–the various combinations of horses and carriages. Unusual turnouts have also been of interest to me. As part of a challenge from a Canadian friend, Gerard Paagman, to do an unusual turnout with horses, I developed "Gloria's Diamond." (See picture to the right.) No record of this turnout has been seen before. It requires driving with six reins in hand. I drove it in 2014 at the Carriage Association of America's Conference at Mullet Hall Equestrian Center on John Island in South Carolina, and it was driven again at the 2015 SICAB, Spain's principal breeder's show. It was with a new pair of young gray PRE's that I also drove in an Attelage de Tradition at SICAB (Salón Internacional del Caballo de Pura Raza Española.)

I have always had a fascination with the horses of Spain. Their classical conformation and their pleasant, tractable demeanor make training them less work. Many horses in this book will be horses of Spanish origin.

I am amazed at the adaptability of a horse to drive in all different configurations. Once trained, horses can work in most positions in a turnout.

The middle picture is of me driving what is called a Unicorn. The bottom is a picture of five horses put to a two-wheeled Cocking Cart. This configuration is still four-in-hand driving because there are four reins in the left hand. Making this the only known time in history this turnout was ever appropriately exhibited to a cocking cart. I do demonstrations and lectures on "How To Do It" and other turnouts. (See my "Equine Elegance" book for more pictures and information on types of turnouts.)

My Passion - Carriage Collector and Educator

The Gloria Austin Carriage Collection formerly resided at The Grand Oaks Resort and Museum in Lady Lake, Florida. It was a collection of over 162 horse-drawn carriages, accompanying artifacts, and art depicting vehicles from around the world. Artifacts of the carriage era were in display cases positioned throughout the museum. Noted as one of the largest most comprehensive collections, it included the only full-state or gala carriage in the United States and the world in private ownership.

My acquisition of each carriage in the collection brought with it a new experience and the desire to know what it would be like to drive each one. Many were in disrepair and, some were fully restored. Those in poor condition went to one of the unique restoration shops in either the U.S. or to Patrick Schroven's shop in Belgium. Since the desire was to drive each carriage, they were restored to drivable condition and as close to original condition as possible, and I knew how each carriage drove. Most of the carriages in the collection were put to horses.

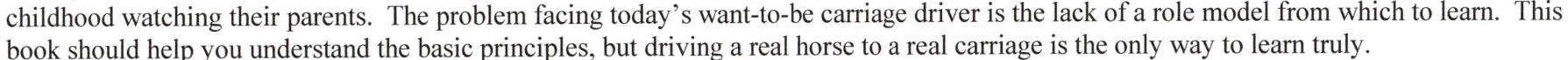

"The Gloria Austin Carriage Collection" book will take you back in time to an era when carriages were used every day for transportation. Years ago driving a carriage and communicating with the horse was something one learned in childhood watching their parents. The problem facing today's want-to-be carriage driver is the lack of a role model from which to learn. This book should help you understand the basic principles, but driving a real horse to a real carriage is the only way to learn truly.

For books, I have written on horses and carriages go to amazon.com or Carriage Association of America's Book Store and ask for books by Gloria Austin.

I Enjoy the Opportunity to Travel and Educate

I now travel and speak about horses and carriages and my history as a four-in-hand driver. I include stories of driving in North America, South America, Europe, and Australia.

Some of the same PowerPoint-assisted lectures developed for educating and training docents and the public at the Grand Oaks Resort and Museum are the ones used when I travel. There are many presentations on both horses and carriages. Among them are:

- Poised for Greatness -The Domestication of the Horse
- Horses, Wheels to Automobiles
- The Horse in America
- Trails, Roads, and Bridges
- Coaches and Coaching
- Shaping Civilization–The Role of the Horse in Human Societies
- Fulfilling Manifest Destiny: The Horse and the American West
- An Up-Close Look at Horses
- Fire Horses
- The Unsung Heroes of World War I
- Tailgating–Its Origins and How to Do the Tailgate Picnic
- Turnout and Pleasure Driving

I believe there should be a discipline at academic institutions called Equine-assisted Education (EAE) to enhance and supplement the learning processes.

I Enjoy Sharing My Knowledge

In 1989, before my travels in Europe, I produced a video with an accompanying booklet for the training of horses to drive. This program included starting guidelines and illustrations.

The Starting Guideline was:

- Prior training
- Age
- Home base
- Getting the horse's attention
- Communicating with your horse in harness which included the use of the voice, bit, reins, and the whip

The Ten Easy Steps were:

- Fit the harness
- Ground drive
    - Move forward
    - Turning
    - Stopping and standing
    - Simulating the cart
    - Simulating pulling and holding back
    - Roadside
- Fit the cart
- Entering the cart
- Walk and halt
- Trot and walk and halt
- Trotting straight & turns
- Varying gaits–extension and collection
- Backing
- Pleasures of driving

This video is no longer available, but it sold with the booklet (pictured to the right) in 1989.

Books I Have Written

The Horse, History, and Culture - A brief commentary and picture log of our 6,000 years of history with the domesticated horse.

Horse Basics 101 - A review of the fundamental information that all horse owners should know.

A Glossary of Harness Parts - A simple glossary to help unravel the terminology used in driving.

The Gloria Austin Carriage Collection - A portfolio of pictures and information on various types of carriages and the carriage world.

A Drive Through Time - A discussion about a few specific carriages and their use in history.

The Brewster Story–An outline of the Brewster carriage manufacturing and sales businesses.

Equine Elegance - A compilation of pictures of turnouts in settings around the world.

Carriage Lamps - A book to help the reader understand the purpose of lamps and the style and size appropriate for each carriage.

The Golden Carriage and the House of Hapsburg This is the story of an Imperial carriage manufactured by the Armbruster Company of Vienna.

Speak Your Horse's Language: Communicating with the Driving Horse Often in history, the talent of communicating with horses was kept a secret. This book passes many of those secrets on to the carriage driver.

Horses Are Still in My Life

After competing for many years and winning many championships, I can now be seen with my horses on Facebook and at club events, special exhibitions, recreational drives, and educational forums. I own seven "Pura Raza Española" (PRE) horses, or Pure Spanish Horses as they are sometimes called. We call them "The Austin Grays." This breed is one of the oldest in existence. I chose the PRE breed especially for their very good temperament, their gray color, tolerance to heat, tractability, and their willingness to perform.

I drove them at Walnut Hill Farm Driving Competition in 2014, and we appeared at the prestigious Newport Coaching Weekend in Rhode Island in 2015. Before they were imported to the United States, I drove them to several venues in Spain.

Each horse has its temperament. Horses are trained in a pair with an experienced horse initially. They are then moved to driving single and are put under saddle. Then, the horses are returned to a pair and are driven as four. During the training process, they go in all positions–leader, wheeler; left, right. When we take them to events, they are driven in the position where they perform their best.

They travel to destinations like Aiken, South Carolina; Southern Pines, North Carolina; Mullet Hall, South Carolina; Kentucky Horse Park, Lexington, Kentucky; Arcadia, Maine; and Chadds Ford, Pennsylvania.

When not traveling, I can be seen driving four—in—hand every day at the Gloria Austin Stables in Central Florida. The regular use of horses is very important. The owner or presenter of the horses has to drive them regularly, so they become what I call "your horses"- meaning they have to understand your reinsmanship, your voice and your way of doing things. The driver and horse have to work together to establish optimal performance.

Understanding the Horse's Mind & Behavior

The Entertainment World
Real and Imagined Horse Behavior

The entertainment world has been full of stories about horses and their real and imagined deeds. This unique creature has drawn the attention of fans of the circus, television, film, literature, and the theater. "The Warhorse," a recent play, and then a Steven Spielberg movie told a heroic story. Historical accounts of horses bring doctors home late at night while the exhausted medical man was asleep in his carriage. Many adults and children are fascinated with this animal and have stories to tell about the wonders of a horse. Even those with no direct knowledge, are enthralled with the sight and wonderment of the horse.

How can horses do wondrous things? How can some people get the horse to perform in talented ways and many others marvel at what they see?

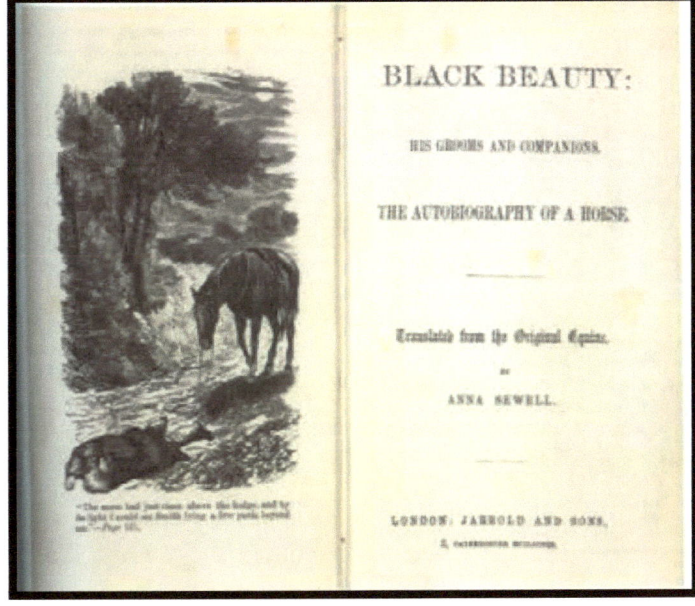

The Real Horse is not a Machine

For most of human history, horses have been the major force in developing our civilized technological world. Even today, man is engineering a mechanical electronically controlled horse to take advantage of the attributes of this four-legged animal. "Kinesiology" is the term associated with the study of human and non-human body movement. There are merits to understanding the biomechanics of the horse and applying it to make a horse-like machine.

"Anthrozoology" is the term associated with the study of the interactive relationship between humans and non-humans, like the horse. Anthrozoology is what we are primarily interested in in this book. How do we relate to horses to get them to do something for us?

The real horse is not like a car or any other machine. It is a living, breathing creature with senses that require an interactive talent and system of communication beyond the "on-off" button and a joystick.

The horse can see, feel, smell, hear, taste, and sense the world; consequently, we must develop a system of asking and getting the reactions we need to control such a large animal for our work or our pleasure.

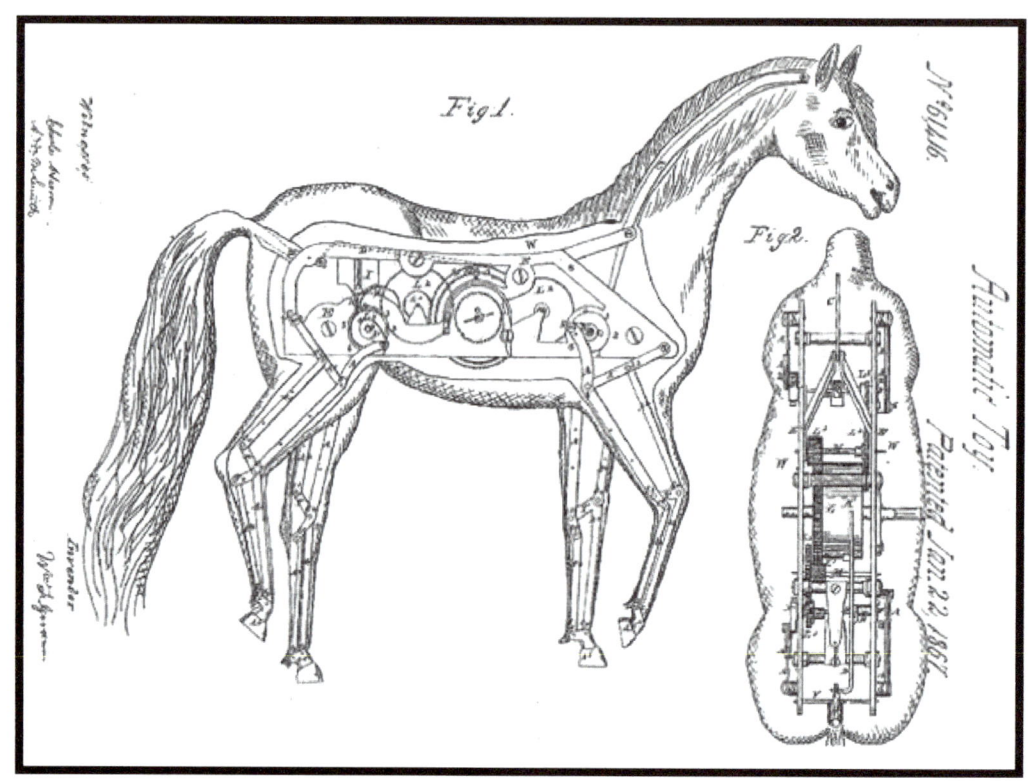

Secrets of Communication

To start learning the secrets of communication is to understand that throughout the evolutionary history of the horse, it has been an animal of prey. Its speed and quick response have allowed it to survive. That is why the horse sleeps standing up with its locking patella. They lie down for only about 20 minutes every two days. Their companions usually stand nearby to give warning of danger.

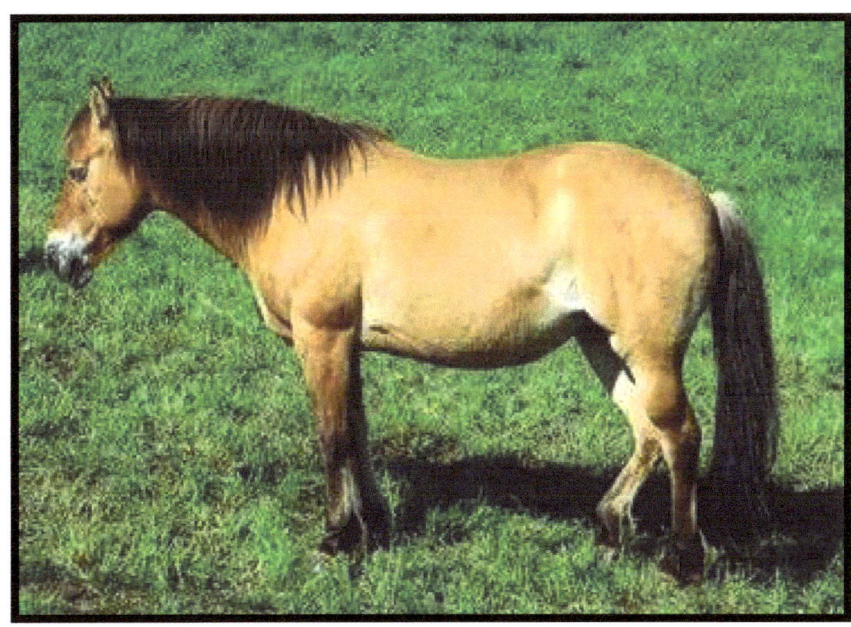

Those that could be on their feet for a quick escape were the ones to survive and produce another generation. As a browsing and then grazing animal, "flight" has been its primary means of survival. Fear is inherent in horses, with varying levels of intensity and behavioral reactions. Bolting, wheeling and then running are not uncommon. Some horses halt and freeze in place. Much of what we do with horses today is to help them not to fear things they perceive as scary, so they do not take flight; so that they take us around in our carriages safely.

Each horse is unique in personality, so each has a different tolerance and reaction. We have to learn the nature of the horse and how to talk to this large, powerful and fast horse.

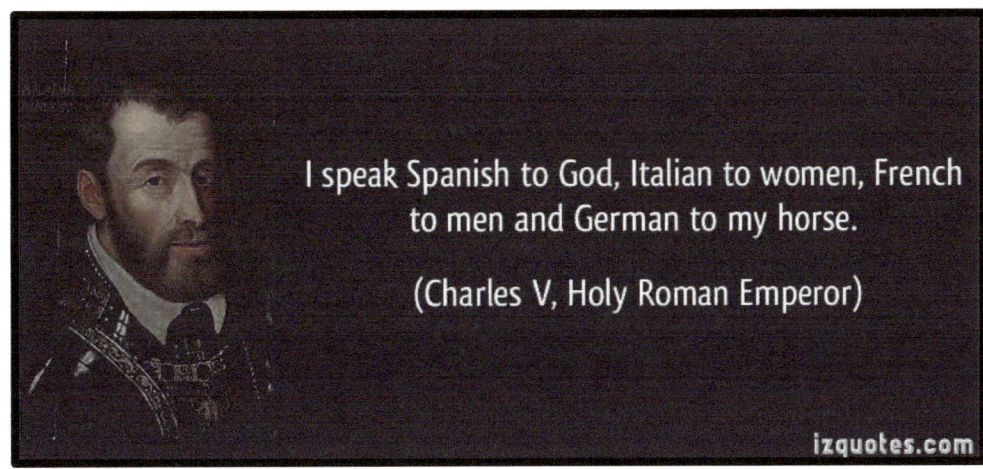

Fight-or-Flight Instinct

"Predation and evolution have shaped the horse's behavior. The horse is an herbivore and prey animal. Flight is its defense. The horse prefers to turn and run away from a perceived threatening situation. This flight reaction to fear is what provides the horse owner a challenge when riding or driving."

The initial response and subsequent reactions are triggered to create a boost of energy. The horse's body will produce glucose, and the circulation of cortisol will turn fatty acids into the energy the body needs to respond. Other chemicals in the body prepare the horse for action, which accelerates the heart and lung action.

Blood flow to the muscles diverts blood flow to other parts of the body. Muscle tension increases which may also speed up blood clotting.

The driver's challenge is to expose the horse to scary things and situations (or a perceived threat) to help the horse reduce these and other reactions. Horses have many of the same physiological changes in their bodies as we do - increased heart rate and the production of chemicals. We must remain calm and convince the horse there is no need for flight and no need for speed, except when asked.

Francis Burton gave a much more detailed explanation in Chapter 7 "The Horse World" from "Ultimate Horse Care," published by Ringpress Books, 1999; ISBN: 1860541860.

A Social Animal

Working in our favor is the horse's social ability. It loves being with other horses and horses have survived in herds for a millennium. They are gregarious and have a pecking order which, in the process of training and communicating, allows us to take advantage of these attributes. We want to be their herd leader and the top in the pecking order so we can direct its behavior through effective communication.

It appears that horses in the wild bond with one another; they like touch; they like hanging out with one another. Those of us that drive pairs or multiples know how much easier it is to drive two horses than to drive one. We take the horse's buddy with him to help them stay together and stay with us rather than running off. Horses seem less tense when with their companions.

Stallions that compete for a mate, on the other hand, often dislike sharing a job with a partner. They have to be carefully trained not to bite or kick or breed a companion at inappropriate times. Many cultures do not believe in castrating stallions, so these people develop specialized skills that are needed to drive stallions successfully.

I advise driving castrated male horses (geldings) in a pair or multiple turnouts. Remember I like to make my life with horses easy, and it is easiest to work with a gelding.

Pecking Order

Understanding this sociability of horses will aid in working with the domesticated horse. They enjoy being part of a herd and have used this to protect themselves in the wild. They bond with other horses and can bond with humans. They seem to enjoy this association.

When in a group, horses have a "pecking order" and humans can learn who the leader of the group is by observing the body language of the horse. This association varies according to the members of the group. When the animals in the group change, the pecking order of the group is changed. When the dominant horse is removed, the number two horse does not necessarily become the leader. A new leader may emerge, and it is his or her buddies that become number 2 and 3, etc. The lesson in life is if your boss changes watch out for a new organizational configuration.

Domestic horses sharing a paddock will often show herd-like behavior. There are usually one or two dominant horses who boss the others around. If some choice grazing or feeding is going on, the dominant ones will grab it first, chasing the others away.

Once the pecking order is established in a herd and everyone has space, it is rare that those horses bite or kick one another.

Horses respond to a leader and take direction from the one they like, using their body language on the part of both individuals. This is most evident at feeding time.

Horses have 11 cycles to their day vacillating between feeding, resting and playing. Play is another time you can observe pecking order.

When at rest, there is usually one horse that stands watch to give warning when there is an imminent danger. At this horse's warning, the others are on their feet, off and running.

Horse to Horse Communication

Horses communicate with one another mainly through body language. As a prey animal, they do not give off much noise even when directing friends or attacking their enemies. In the wild, the noise would reveal their position, so they have developed mostly as a silent animal.

Most aggression is done with flattened ears, flared nostrils, and a swishing tail. Biting is a particularly bad form of aggression and particularly dangerous if directed toward a human.

Kicking or threatening a kick is also the horse's way of expression.

This aggressive or dominant behavior is typical for alpha leaders in a herd of horses. Aggression is often manifested around food, or it may just be whenever we enter their personal space. Horses often outweigh humans by 1,000 pounds, so this behavior has to be curbed.

Quick and concise reprimands for bad behavior are warranted.

Often the issue of disrespect grows over time as your horse discovers that he can be disrespectful and get away with it. Horses will challenge you every day to determine if you are worthy to be their leader. It will start with the little things until it turns into a major problem over time.

Mutual Grooming

Horses spend time mutual grooming, mostly with a couple of close friends. Although, all horses in a herd, or sharing a paddock, will mutually groom every horse in their herd at some time.

This understanding of mutual grooming can be used with driving horses if a horse becomes nervous when standing in harness. An on-the-ground handler/groom can scratch the withers and sometimes calm the horse.

The mouth of a horse is sensitive. Therefore, a horse that is very upset in the harness can be brought back to reality by a handler shaking the bit in the horse's mouth. This can get the attention of the horse back on the presence of the groom. A see-sawing motion of the bit through the reins can sometimes do the same.

Horses are Dependent on Mothers

Early on, the dam (or mother) teaches her foal to behave by using her body language. Prey animals must start learning from birth. In the wild, birthing might attract the predator so moving early in life meant survival. Mares and foals bond early on and move quickly together. The foal learns early on to watch the body language of the mother.

We take advantage of these early lessons to train horses in a round pen where you or your favorite horse whisperer get the young horse to respond to your body signals before directing them through touch or other means.

Mares teach their foals early on in life to respect them as the leader. The foals will act like there is a lead line attached to their mother and stay close to her side.

A good test to see if your horse respects you as his leader is to walk around without a lead rope in an enclosed area. If he chooses to follow you, he understands that you are the alpha leader just as his mother was. If he does not follow you, continue with groundwork exercises and hustling their feet. Horses are natural followers. The more you move their feet, the more respect they will have for you, and thus be willing to follow you.

Respect for humans cannot be obtained overnight. Respect is a process that takes time. It is not only something to teach your horse, but you must learn the feel and timing of how to keep a horse out of your space and move their feet while not moving yours. This takes practice before it will become second nature. Give it time, be consistent and you will notice improvements every day. Horses don't ever stay the same. Every day they either get a little better or a little worse. If you maintain that respect and improve upon it, your horse's behavior will improve every day.

"People Need People and Horses Need Horses,"

Horses suffer if not within sight of another horse. If you pasture a horse alone, make sure he has a clear vision of another horse, or they will develop problems such as depression and sometimes stop eating. This is why racehorses that are isolated in stalls were often given a goat as a companion. The expression "get your goat" comes from the theft of the goat to cause distress to the racehorse so it might be exhausted before the race.

We take advantage of their natural or innate characteristics to "need a leader" by putting ourselves in a position to direct the horse. Because of their size and strength advantage over that of the human, it is impossible to force a horse to cooperate. Don't try or ever get in a fight with a horse. You will lose. Our leadership is usually done through bonding, trust, communication and cueing with what we call aids. In the case of driving: the reins, voice, and whip.

Horses may exhibit aggression toward their partner in a pair as they get close to their home stable. Stallions are territorial and some carriage driving stallions, and even geldings will exhibit aggression toward a partner when close to their home stable.

Don't take all acts of aggression or disobedience personally. Horses are not out to get you or get revenge. They just have not been taught respect or do not understand what they should be doing. Sometimes they just have a lapse.

Some horses are not salvageable. Horses that fall to the ground when pressured or are extremely aggressive with their mouths and biting may not be worth your time. The mouthy horse is sometimes useful in doing tricks which require grabbing a cloth or other items–not a person. These horses have to have special handlers and often appear in performing acts.

I recommend not feeding a horse from your hand to discourage a horse from seeking attention with its mouth. If you give your horse a snack or treat, place the treat in its feeding bucket.

The Horse's Memory

Equine cognitive science is a fairly new discipline. Horse owners have known for years that this animal can remember things from its past. Horses that have had bad experiences seem to remember and fear certain objects, people, or actions. The challenge to the trainer and handlers is to reinforce good behavior in the learning process so that the horse will perform the desired behavior years later. The horse's temperament in this process of remembering is still unknown.

Although horses remember well, they don't hold grudges, and neither should you. If a nip is directed at you, and you reprimand in return, once that exchange is over, it's all water under the bridge. Horses don't have the same emptional structure that humans have. So don't feel bad reprimanding a horse. They do not take things personally. You have to earn their respect.

Horses seem to be sequential learners and will remember the last in a series, so always end your exercise session with a positive experience with an activity the horse does well. Therefore, it is very important to recognize and correct unwanted behaviors before these behaviors become bad habits.

I like a quote from Pat Parelli: "If your horse says no, you have either asked the wrong question or asked the question wrong." Not all horses are alike. What works for one horse might not work for another. It is the trainer's/handler's job to figure out what and how to ask for each horse.

Horses need a vacation sometime, just like we do. Sometimes time off is helpful to renew you and your horse's work time together. Don't worry they will not forget what you have taught them.

Horses also need to have an interesting environment, so they don't become dull.

The Horse's Body Language

Communication is a two-way street. The better the horsemen and women are at reading the body language of the horse; the better they are at detecting the mood or response of the horse.

The ears, eyes, body posture and tail position are four of the primary indicators.

The horse's senses are well developed. They also have keen senses of touch, smell, and hearing–all of which we must understand.

Here are some things to look for when reading the horse's silent language:

- Tense, stiff muscles mean the horse is hurting, scared, or stressed.
- Trembling means he or she is chilled or fearful.
- Reaching out and touching you with the muzzle means curiosity, or biting may mean they are looking for a snack.
- Smelling, listening, or seeing is also the way a horse recognizes its handler.
- Moving toward a fixed object or another horse often means insecurity.
- Moving rear end side-to-side means it might kick, particularly when accompanied by pinned ears and a swishing tail.
- Pinned ears mean, "Stay away, I don't want you close."
- A tail raised above the back means excitement.
- A tail clamped close to its body means nervousness or stress.
- A rapid swishing of the tail means discomfort from flies or other irritation and may mean the horse is about to kick or buck.

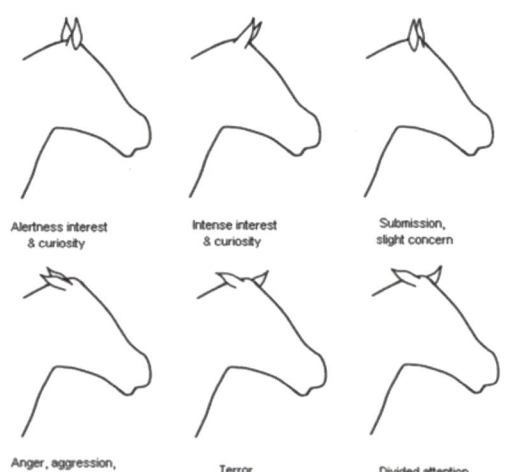
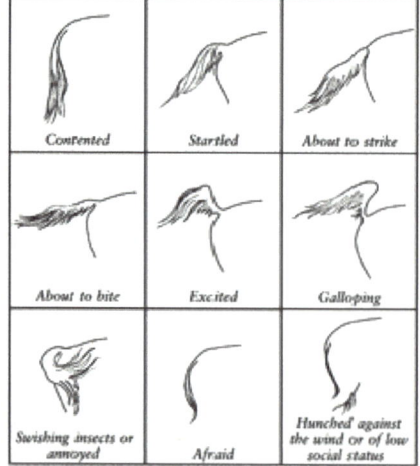

Reading the Whole Body

Signs or gestures of discomfort are looking away, head movement, excessive twitching on the skin, leg movement, flared nostrils, heavy breathing, and tail swishing.

Gestures of comfort are: lowered head, yielding the head in the direction of the trainer, reaching out with the muzzle to smell the person, sniffing, actual touching of the muzzle on the person, chewing and licking of the lips, standing quietly as the person moves about the horse, and a relaxed body posture with head lowered.

Our goal is to get the horse to like us, trust that we are not a threat, and show signs of comfort. All of this takes time spent with the horse. Our goals are for the horse to be calm and thus the handler has to remain calm and react in ways that solicit relaxed comfort.

I can remember early in my driving career someone saying to me, "You have a happy horse." Never having thought of it in that way, I was proud to respond, "Yes, they seem calm, relaxed and comfortable."

Comfort is more than just emotional comfort, but the physical comfort that we all feel with properly fitting shoes and clothes. The horse must have a properly fitting harness, be shod properly, and have a bit that fits the horse's mouth and does not cause pain. Comfort is also vested in the hands and demeanor of the handler. The horse must believe it is not going to be hurt or abused and think of its handler as a friend.

Bonding often occurs with just proximity or juxtaposition. Just being and working with a person or animal creates a bond as long as there is no threat from the other. Men or women "fall in love" with their workmates. Men on a team bond as they respond and react to one another on the field of play.

Horses also respond to those who spend time with them. If not familiar, they seek out an understating of the person they see, hear and smell, most often. Horsemen and women don't get the rewards of training their equine companions without spending time together with their horse(s).

Horses are Running Machines

Horses are running machines with their biomechanics and digestive systems structured to facilitate speed. They can gallop up to 35 MPH for short distances, and they can sustain the trot of 8-10 MPH over longer distances. When conditioned, they can travel 100 miles in 12 hours. It is not the speed of our modern transportation, but for 6,000 years they were the only thing that could carry man faster than his own two legs on land.

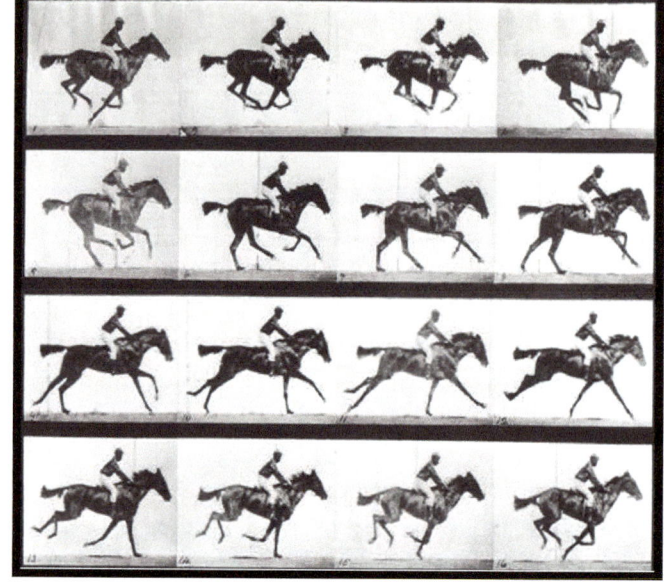

Horse racing is an ancient sport. Its origins date back to about 4500 BCE among the nomadic tribesmen of Central Asia (who first domesticated the horse). Since then, horse racing has flourished as the sport of kings. Thoroughbreds, Standardbreds, and Quarter Horses are often raced here in the USA where leisure and gambling offer people the opportunity to attend horse races at formalized specialty race tracks.

Most people don't realize that horses, as we know them, were not indigenous to the United States. The Spanish introduced horses to the western hemisphere when Queen Isabella of Spain required Columbus to bring horses to the New World.

It was not until the bicycle came along did man have another tool for speed on land. The earliest bicycles were even called Hobby Horses. It was not until the late 1800's that functionally practical bicycles were used.

People Can Read Horse's Emotions

The ears of the horse are probably the greatest indicator of where the horse's attention is focused. The ears can move independently of one another, which means the horse is trying to focus on two things at the same time. The light-colored driving horse on the right has his ears turned in different directions meaning his attention is in two different places.

Elevation of their head beyond its normal position means curiosity or fear. It can also mean excitement. This movement of the head is a way of lining up light receptors in the eye for distant vision as with the horse at the lower right of this page. The raised head can also mean resistance or pain from an ill-fitting or painful bit.

The natural head carriage of a horse is dictated by confirmation and breeding. It is most important to have a bit that is comfortable in a horse's mouth and can be used to signal the horse without causing discomfort.

Lowered or Raised Head

The lowered head can be a good or bad sign. It can be lowered to smell and assess the stability of a surface, or it can be lowered to buck its hindquarters in the air. When teaching a young horse to load in a trailer, a lower head is a good sign that the horse has the common sense to check out where he is to step.

A raised head usually indicates the horse has detected a threat and is trying to line up those light receptors to see something at a distance. Sometimes the head is raised because of excitement, pain or improper training.

A horse can be trained to raise and lower its head with the use of the inside rein. We will discuss this later in the book.

Bearing reins were used quite commonly years ago if there was a need to keep the horse's head in position so it would not lower its head and lose its bridle, to prevent it from grazing, and to keep its bridle and bit from getting caught on the carriage pole or harness of another horse. There are three types of bearing reins: direct, indirect and overhead checkrein. The "overcheck" is still used in Standardbred racing and some breed shows.

Today's driver does not use a bearing rein. It is important that the driving horse is trained to keep its head in position for the work it is performing. I never let a horse in harness lower its head to the point where I cannot see its ears.

Smell

Horses have a very acute sense of smell and use it to interpret the world in ways that are far beyond the capabilities of humans.

Horses also relate to their immediate environment through their sense of smell. They greet each other nose to nose and recognize each other by scent and by sight.

Horses have two different olfactory centers. One is exclusively developed for detecting and analyzing pheromones for determining the reproductive status of other horses.

Horses come to recognize people in the same way. Notice the recognition you get when you approach a horse - the horse reaches out its muzzle to take in your scent by sniffing you.

As with other animals, extending the back of your hand is a good way to let the horse get to know and trust you and accept your presence as a herd mate and not a predator.

Horses greet one another by touching noses and smelling each other's breath. Horses can recognize their handlers 100 paces away by smell.

Equine Behavioral Health Resource Center states "Additionally, while humans rely in large part upon their sight and hearing to understand and participate in the world around them, horses rely on their sense of smell. The equine sense of smell is thousands of times more sensitive than the human counterpart."

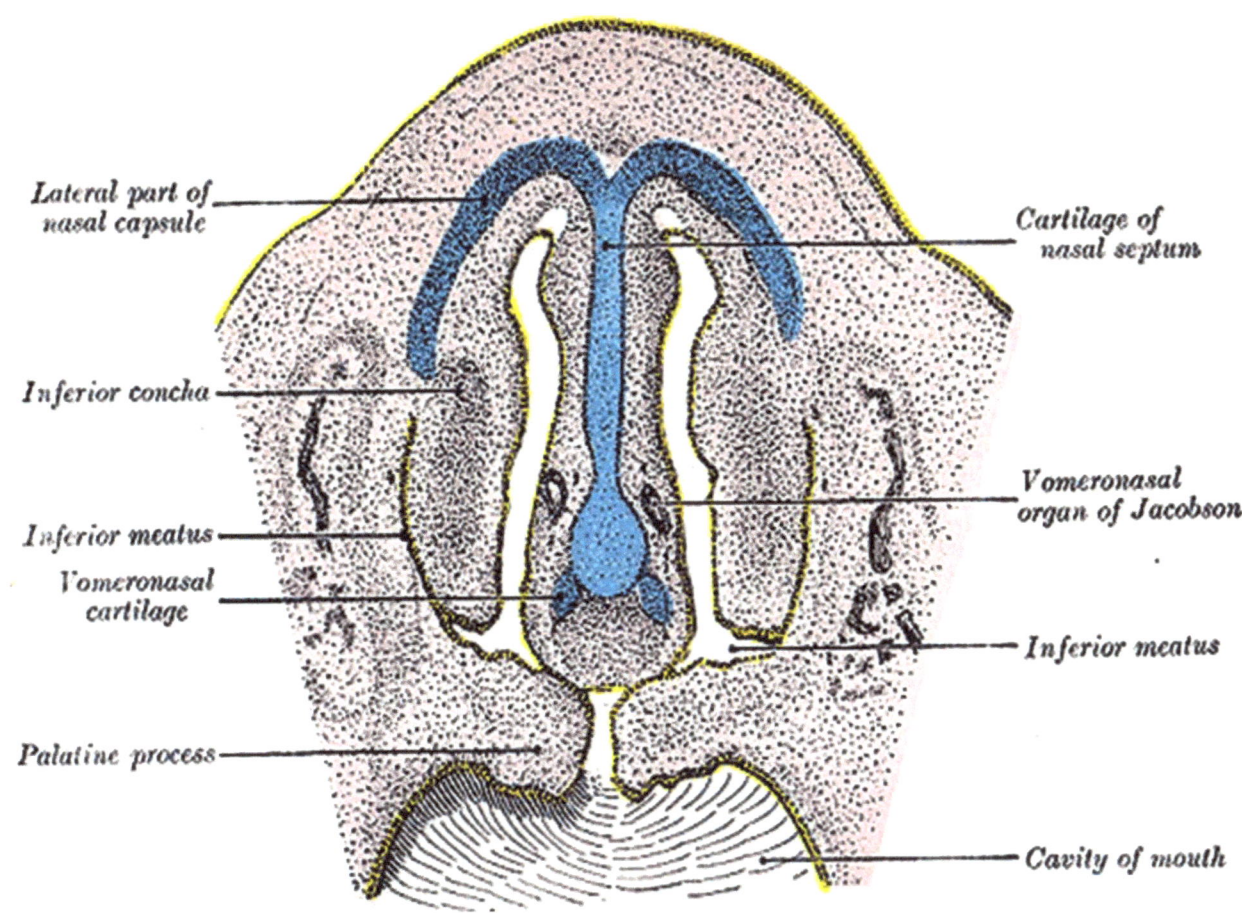

Hearing

The horses with the best hearing that could take flight from a predator were the ones that lived to pass on this genetic trait.

Their ears are funnel-shaped and very mobile. This ability to perceive and process sound quickly and efficiently serves the horse well. Loud and unfamiliar noises can send a horse into flight or a combative attitude if it feels threatened.

Amazingly, a soft, gentle voice that is calm and confident can work wonders with gaining the cooperation of a horse. With their keen sense of hearing, horses respond well to the sound of the human voice. Keep this idea in mind always and especially when you and your horse are in a noisy or frightening environment.

I regularly speak to my horses as their ears tell me they have noticed potential danger. I might say in a soft, gentle voice: "I see it. It's OK."

I might speak in a sharp stern voice if I want them to fear me more than the scary thing at their feet.

I even will speak to people along the roadway if I think the horse might shy at their dog or baby stroller, letting the horse know that I view the person as a friend, not foe.

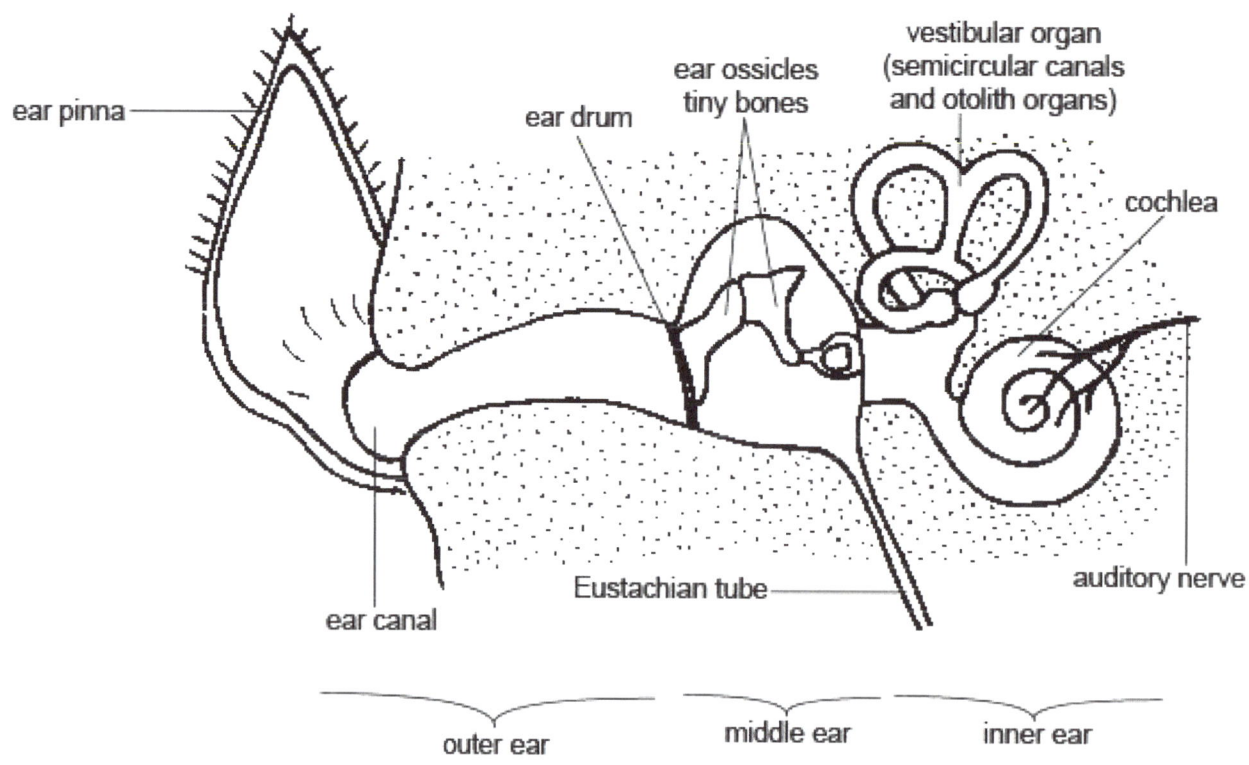

Touch

Horses are seven times more sensitive to touch than humans. That is why the more gifted handlers, once the horse understands cues, can use a very light touch to direct a horse. Often you never see our cues.

Although horse skin is believed to be tough, it has many nerve endings and can sense the tiniest fly landing or buzz near its coat hairs.

Your touch tells your horse, "Hey, I'm your friend," and, in many cases, the horse will return the compliment with a touch or a body language that speaks their intentions.

Its muzzle with its hairs is of great help to the horse in understanding its environment and greeting other horses and people.

The EquiMed staff tells us, "A gentle touch tells the horse that you mean it no harm."

The sensitivity of the horse's mouth and balance in its head and neck, allows us to place a bit in its mouth and with the lightest of tugs give it a queue to place its feet inches to the right or left.

Fuego XII, owned by Miguel de Cardenas, was born in 1998 and is seen ridden by the Spanish equestrian, Juan Manuel Muñoz Diaz, in the sport of dressage. When you watch them perform, you can tell this horse and rider have formed a close bond - they are friends!

Sight

Sight is probably the most important of the equine senses. They have much better night vision than humans do. Drivers depended on the horses night vision to take advantage of the reduced traffic at night.

Horses have developed eyes on the sides of their heads to see impending danger, even when grazing. They have both monocular and binocular vision and are well-suited to see at night.

With eyes on the side of its head, the horse can see almost 360 degrees, although a blind zone exists behind and underneath its body, and a little in front of its forehead.

Because of the blind spots, it is important not to approach a horse from the rear unless the horse knows you are there, and it is also important to approach a horse at an angle when approaching from the front.

When approaching a driving horse with blinders from behind, such as a groom might when dismounting the carriage to check for traffic at an intersection, it is important to have the groom speak softly to the horse to alert the horse of his or her presence as not to startle the horse.

Horses have the largest eyes of the land mammals. Having both monocular and binocular vision allows them to see danger when grazing. Monocular vision, which allows the horse to watch in front of him with one eye and in back of him with the other, is why the horse must be trained to accept things on one side and then on the other side.

Horses and humans have what could best be called a camera-type eye. Light passes through the lens and focuses the image on the retina at the back of the eye–much like a camera lens throwing an image on to a piece of film.

The eye's curved retina is linked to the optic nerve, which transmits information about the visual environment to the brain.

Their light receptors are in the center of their eyes, so they often move their heads up and down to line up receptors to view objects.

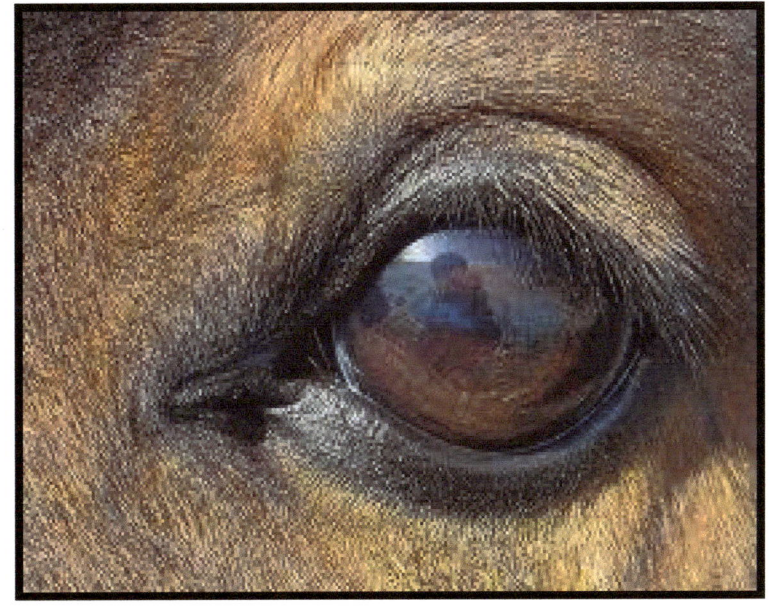

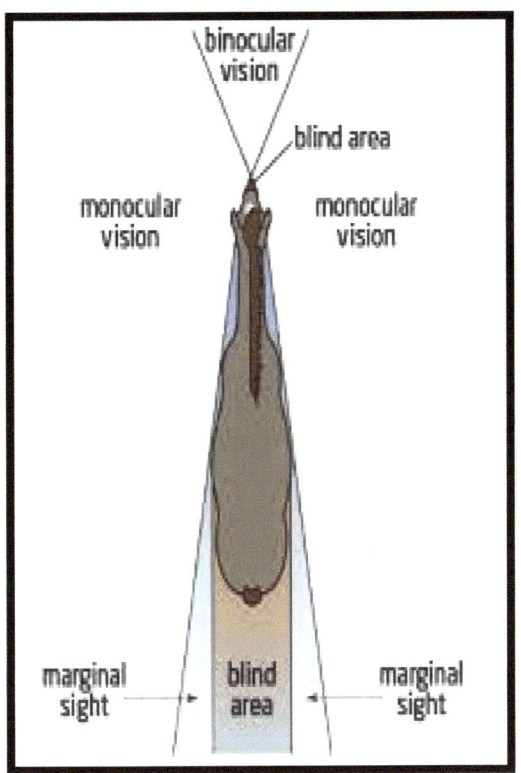

The Brain of the Horse

The International Society for Equitation Science (www.equitationscience.com), combined with an ever-growing interest in behavioral research at many universities, has caused a wave within the horse industry, bringing trainers and scientists together. That's why well-known horseman and clinician Martin Black has paired up with Dr. Stephen Peters, a neuropsychologist who specializes in brain functioning, to digest information about the horse's brain and natural anatomy. Their book and accompanying DVD, "Evidence-Based Horsemanship," pairs science with empirical insight to recommend the best practices for horse owners.

This duo suggests the following: "The horse's brain is about the size of a large grapefruit and is proportionately 1/650th of its body weight. In comparison, the human brain is about 1/50th of our body weight. Current research still supports that the brain ratio to body mass reflects a level of cognitive skills, thus giving humans more capacity to think. However, this doesn't mean the horse is dumb; it simply thinks and processes slightly different from humans. The horse relies more on instinct and group decisions than individual thought.

One of the most important structures of the horse's brain, the cerebellum, plays a role in controlling balance and head and eye movements. For the horse's life, the cerebellum will act as a library for storing all learning about physical movement.

A horse that is in a state of fight-or-flight tends to be emotionally unstable (easily disturbed/stressed out easily/sensitive/nervous/angry/anxious). In this frame of mind, he is unable to learn new things from the trainer. The reptilian brain (consisting of the brain stem and cerebellum) is concerned with survival and body maintenance. Digestion, reproduction, circulation, breathing, and the "fight-or-flight" response are all reptilian brain functions. This seems to be developed in horses.

When a horse is more at ease, he tends to be emotionally stable (calm/secure/confident/relaxed). In this frame of mind, he can learn new things from the trainer. The second layer is the limbic system. It includes the amygdala and hippocampus and involves emotion and memory. The limbic system concerns itself with primitive activities related to food, sex, and bonding. It is responsible for memories of behaviors connected to agreeable and disagreeable experiences. In humans, these are called emotions. This area also is developed in horses.

The third layer is the neocortex or cerebral cortex. It makes up most of the human brain. Language, speech, and writing are all possible because of this layer. It is also where we perform abstract thinking, organize things, categorize ideas, reason, and multi-task. The large human neocortex versus the underdeveloped version of the equine is one of the most notable differences between the way humans and horses operate.

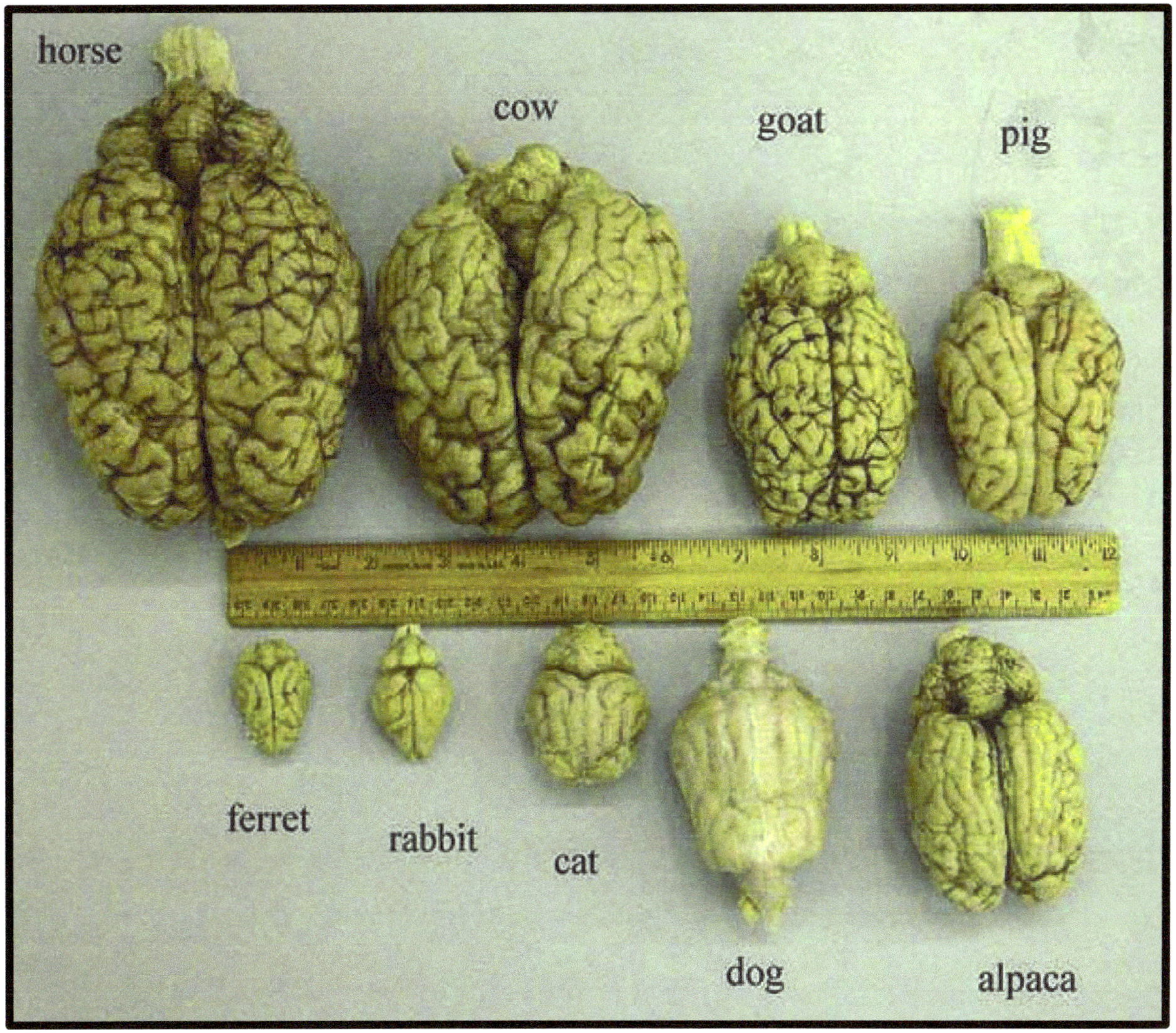

"Brain specimens of these animals were donated and made plastic by the College of Veterinary Medicine at the University of Tennessee Knoxville. Please note: No animals were killed in this exhibit."

According to the Equine Behavioral Health Resource Center: "Many scientists believe there is a correlation between brain weight and intelligence. The adult human brain weighs approximately three pounds.

A cat's brain weighs about a third of a pound. Dog brains weigh about three-fourths of a pound. The brain of the horse is the size of a human child's and weighs from one and a half pounds to two pounds. Oddly enough, although smaller, the horse's brain is similar to our own with a few differences. The most important difference is that much of the human brain is used for fine-motor skills and language development, while most of the horse's brain is used for analyzing information received from the environment.

The Senses and Proximity

So, you may have guessed it by now, the senses of the horse and our proximity to the horse are the foundation to bonding, trust, and communication. These senses of touch, vision, smell, and hearing all produce a partnership of cooperation.

Never punish the horse for using its senses to detect danger, but help the horse in coping with its fears and reactions to scary and unfamiliar things. The horse's repeated exposure to things that the human knows is not harmful will help the horse overcome its fear. The more experiences the horse has and the better the understanding of its environment, the less their unfounded fear.

We spend hours exposing a horse to scary things and over time, the horse will trust that if you think it's OK and will not hurt, then they will not be scared. I will even talk to the horse in a soothing tone to acknowledge that I have seen what it sees. I will even say, "good watching, I see it, it's OK."

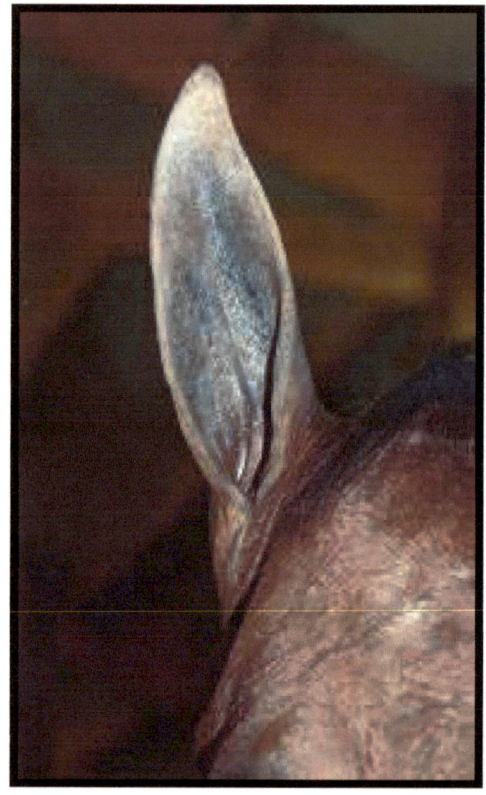

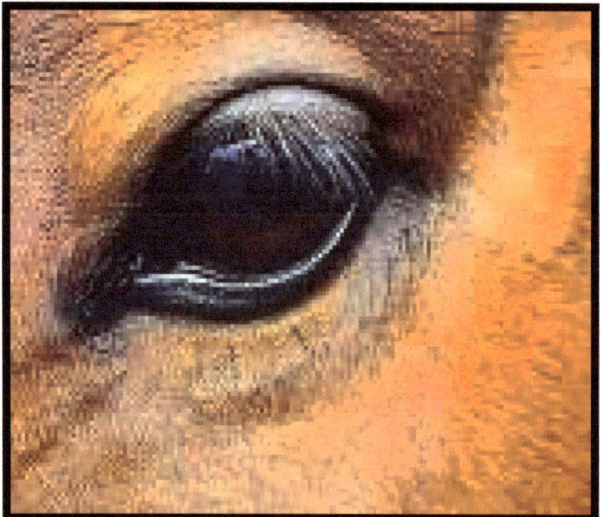

To Review:

- Horses are prey animals, not predators.
- Horses are social herd animals. They seek companionship.
- Their reaction generally to fear is flight.
- Horses have a hierarchy in the herd and like structure and routine.
- If left in the wild, horses have a routine to their daily activities of eating, resting and playing.
- They like a leader and have a pecking order depending on the individuals in the herd. They have their horse friends and have others they don't like.
- Horses communicate among themselves mainly through body language and watch for visual clues from other horses.
- You must teach a horse to respect your space.
- Horses are tractable and willing to accept man as his boss and take direction from a person.
- Horses can read and sense the demeanor of persons with whom they are familiar.

CHOOSING A HORSE

We Want a Happy Horse

The driver wants a happy horse that is calm, comfortable and:

- Stands still - this is probably the most important of our desires.
- Moves straight at the walk and at the trot.
- Halts when asked.
- Trots at three ground covering strides.
- Bends its neck and moves laterally in either direction.
- Reins back only a directed number of steps.
- Canters when signaled. This gait is infrequently used and should, as with all other gaits, only be done upon command.

It is most helpful if a driver chooses a horse that has the conformation and disposition for the job of the trot and pulling a carriage. This requires a horse that is up-headed with a long enough neck to move the neck and head out of the way of the shoulder as it moves forward at the trot.

The basic nature of some horses tends to be calm and have a tractable personality. There are other attributes drivers should look for, such as having leaders in a four that are fearless and brave. Wheelers need to be hardworking followers. These characteristics are difficult to assess without trying a horse in the various positions. Some horses prefer to work alone, and others prefer to work beside one another in a pair or as multiples.

One of the most commonly misunderstood problems in having a horse with a proper disposition is the relationship between feeding practices and equine behavior; and the relationship between work and feeding practices. Horse management is critical to optimal performance.

Purchasing a Safe Horse

If you are a less than experienced driver, you will want to take a trusted professional with you. It is important that the adviser does not influence you to buy a horse that is too much horse for you to handle. You have to be comfortable with the horse. Don't just buy the pretty horse or the one that is the color you have always wanted. That pretty gray horse might not be the best for you. Most professionals want you to meet with success, so their insights are important.

Remember, you are looking for a horse that has the disposition and the conformation for the job. Some dealers, breeders, and private individuals specialize in selling carriage driving horses or ponies. Try to secure the reputation of the seller before your visit.

Secure a testimony from those who might be former owners or know of this horse. Reputations seem to travel in the community of carriage driving. I often arrive suddenly to look at a horse I have expressed interest in, so there is no opportunity for the horse to be drugged before my arrival.

Sometimes a retiring driver may have an experienced horse that has won prizes in your style of driving. Remember that breed show driving, pleasure driving, and combined driving are quite different. Therefore, try to look for a horse that is schooled in the discipline you are most interested.

Soundness examinations can be done by the professional with you, or if the horse is high priced, you may want to have a veterinarian examine the horse you like before spending a large sum of money.

Remember that horses are unique individuals and respond differently in the hands of each person.

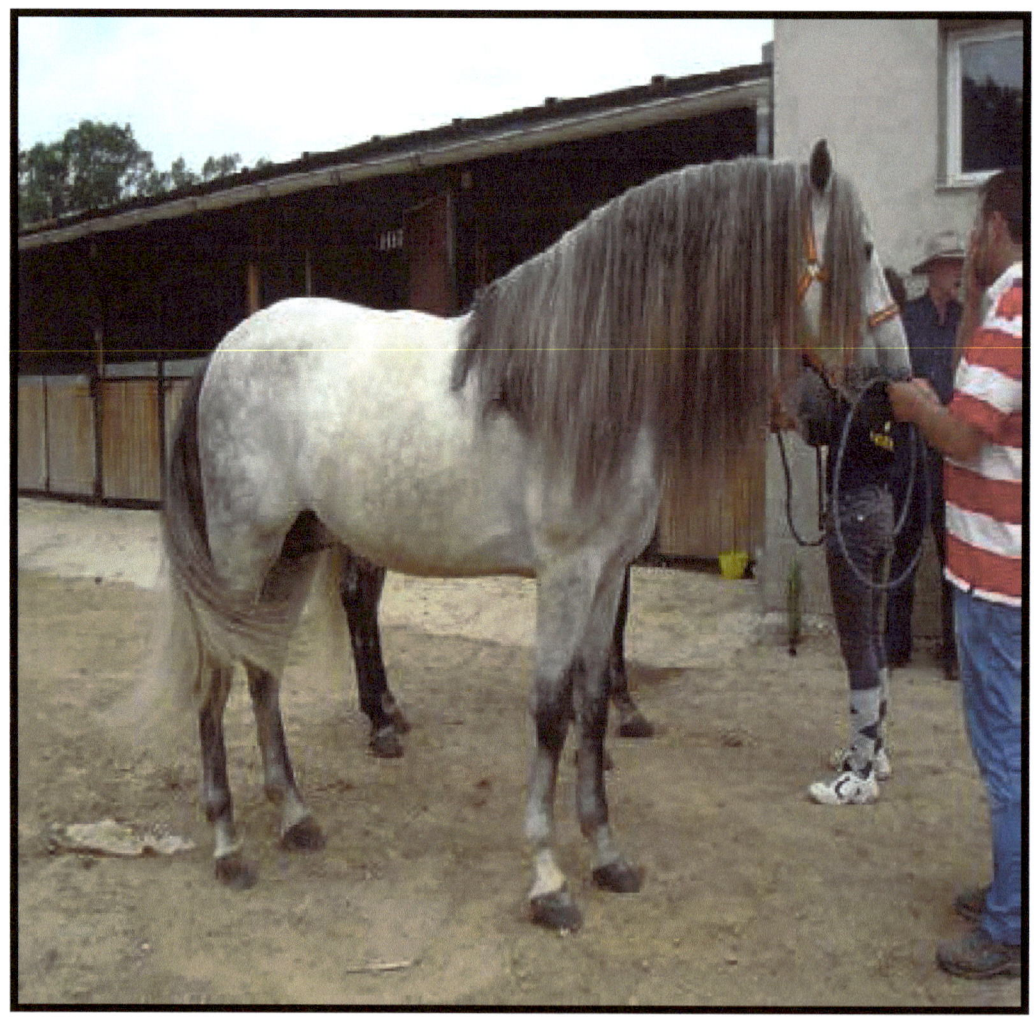

Pre-Purchase Examination

The first step is to look at the horse standing tied. Is it calm and comfortable as you and others approach? Remember always to approach the front shoulder at a 45-degree angle. You can start the touch-part of the exam by first touching the shoulder, then neck and I then like to pet the horse on the head and then touch the pole and ears of the horse. I don't like horses that are head shy. I am short and need the horse not to resist bridling. The horse should stay relaxed and quiet while you are doing this. If the horse tolerates you touching its ears, it should be accustomed to bridling.

I also check for sight by looking into the eye for spots or blemishes. You can move your hand quickly toward the eye (without touching the eye or the hairs out around the eye) to see if the horse blinks. If the horse blinks, it is usually a sign of sightedness.

Ask for the horse to be stood so you can look at it from in front, the side and behind so that you can examine the legs and feet for correct alignment. If you are interested in driving, you should understand proper common conformational characteristics which are outlined in many places. You can lift the feet and examine the hoof and bottom of the foot. The horse should willingly let you pick up its hooves. If timid about this process, ask the owner/handler of the horse to do this for you.

Common Unsoundnesses

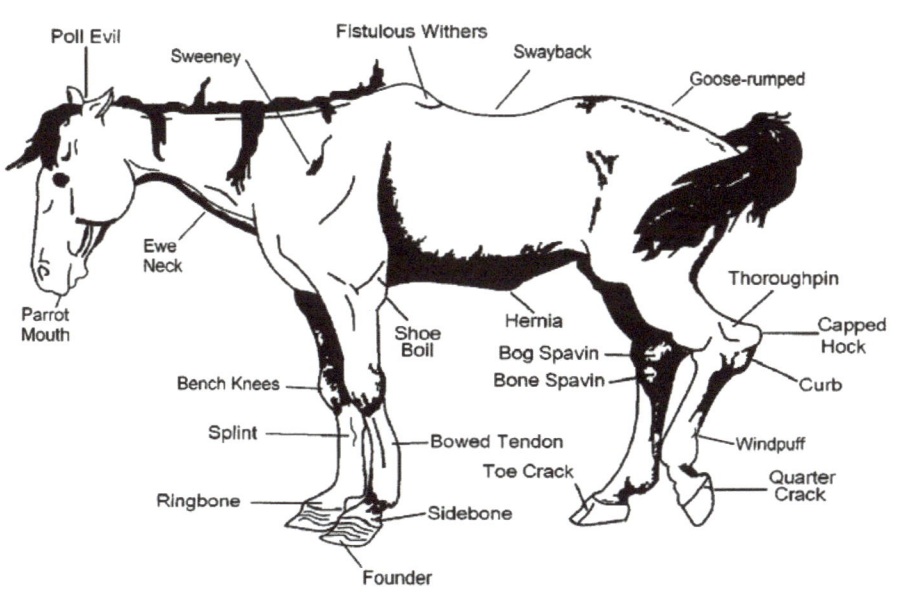
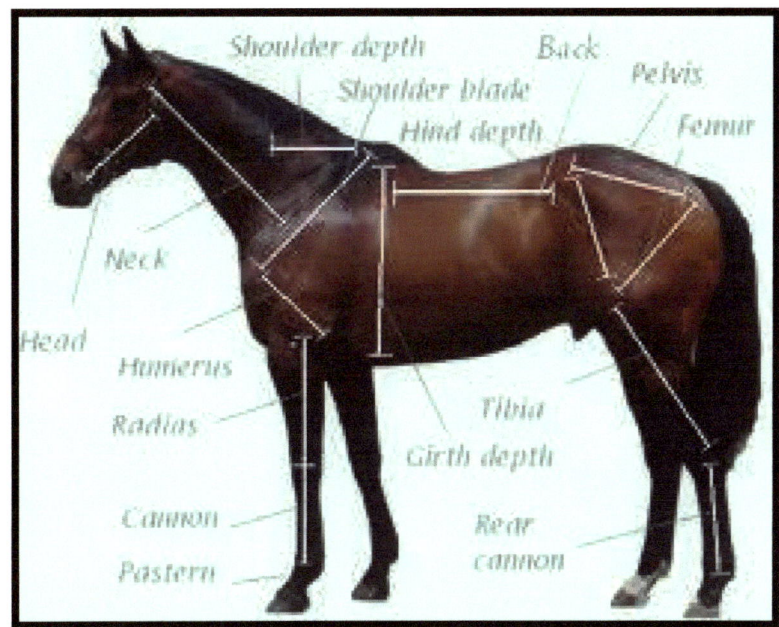

Ask the owner/handler to walk the horse on a hard surface towards you as you stand 30 to 50 feet in front of the horse and then turn the horse and walk away from you. You should be watching for lameness and footfalls. The horse's legs should track straight, and the feet should land square with no rotation as the foot strikes the ground. Some horse's feet will track too close, and some are pigeon toed or splay outward. Do this again and observe from the side to see how much the horse is tracking up from behind into the space vacated by the front foot. Repeat this procedure at the trot. Request the horse be turned in both directions and watch to see that the horse is not gimpy on the turn which can indicate problems.

If you know how to do a flexion test, do it. The flexion test can let you know something about the joints. If the horse is a costly horse, you will want to have an impartial veterinarian examine the horse with the proper tools and even take x-rays of the joints and feet.

If you are buying a horse not yet trained for driving, I would depend heavily on the judgment of a trusted professional because you will probably be asking that person to train or help you train the horse.

Let us assume you are out to buy a driving a horse that is already driving. I prefer to buy a young three or four-year-old horse that has been handled by professionals. I like it if they are already started under the hands of a quality professional that already knows what I am looking for and believes the horse is suitable. It is best to buy a driving horse that is a bit older with no bad habits that have been driven in a variety of places in a variety of circumstances.

I first ask the owner/trainer to harness and drive the horse, that way I can observe the ground manners and how it acts during these procedures. I then watch as the horse is driven to look for its stride at the walk and then the trot. I watch to see that it stands quietly and doesn't anticipate or rush into its gaits and transitions. I watch that the horse travels straight and also if it is willing to bend and turn in the direction of the turn. I watch to see if he understands lateral movements. I also watch for signs of resistance to the bit or counter bending.

If all goes well, I ask the professional that I brought with me to drive the horse or horses, and if that goes well, I will take the reins to see if the horses are light on the bit and are responsive to my reinsmanship. I appreciate horses that keep an even cadence in the turn and up and down inclines. Minor things I can correct, but major things like rearing, resistance to the bit, and over flexing are difficult to correct and do not buy a kicking horse.

If possible, ask to see the horse loaded in the trailer.

The Driving Horse's Conformation

The driving horse must be up-headed, so the neck and head are out of the way of the forearm at the trot. The neck has to be long enough and the throat thin enough for the horse to be properly in frame - where a line perpendicular to the ground from the forehead passes just behind the nostril. The position of the head and neck needs to be such that the driving horse is not over flexed. Such flexion can obstruct the trachea or windpipe. However, the head and neck should be flexed enough to bring the horse into balance over his four feet for the trot.

Ideally, the pelvis of a driving horse should be long enough to give a large area for attachment of the propulsive muscles, and it should have a moderate slope to facilitate tilting the pelvis, lowering the haunches and moving the hind legs forward under the horse's body.

The muscles of the back are easily seen from the driver's position. These muscles must be used, and therefore the back is elevated when the horse has properly engaged the hindquarters. I believe that driving is easier for horses than riding since the saddle and rider interfere with the use of these muscles.

The horse must be as comfortable as possible to enjoy its work. Proper conformation for the trot is essential for the driving horse. The Friesian, Hackney, Gelderlander, and Baroque horses like the Spanish, Lusitano, Lipizzaner and Kladruby are all built for driving and executing the trot.

Cantering breeds of horses like thoroughbreds, quarter horses, and Arabians have their conformation more suited for the canter. It is not that they cannot be driven, but more training and focused work is needed to prepare these horses for the job.

"THERE IS SOMETHING ABOUT THE OUTSIDE OF A HORSE THAT IS GOOD FOR THE INSIDE OF A MAN."
Winston Churchill

Unspoken

"Unspoken Messages" is written by an army veteran about a journey through a cancer diagnosis while walking beside and being taught by animals of all kinds. His cancer is related to two tours in Vietnam a lifetime ago. Richard D. Rowland received over eight years of peace and happiness through his association with the horse and other animals. He describes his metaphysical explorations and his confrontation of the challenge of healing himself from highly invasive cancer.

Dr. Michael Fox, a veterinarian with doctoral degrees in medicine and animal behavior, writes about how animals often play an unrecognized and unappreciated role in our growth and transformation into more humane beings, making us more compassionate and empathic and less self-involved and more aware.

I often think that ballroom dancing and my association with horses makes me a healthier person and I can do as much as I do at my age because of it. I tell the DJ at a local dance club that he does more to preserve the lifestyle and health of the dancers than all the conventional western trained doctors do.

Dr. Fox states that Rowland describes horse to horse and human to horse events as, "Something spiritual, something older than time, some transfer of wisdom or spirit took place through the communication that we witness" like a horse's reaction to the death of another.

"Unspoken Messages" - "Spiritual Lessons I Learned from Horses and Other Earthbound Souls," is just one such account of the transformational effects of our relationship with the horse.

What Happens in People?

Anthrozoology (also known as human–non-human-animal studies or HAS) is the study of the interaction between humans and other animals. Understanding of this relationship may help us to know how to improve our communication with horses.

Equine assisted education and equine assisted therapy seem to be making strides in improving the lives of those with developmental disabilities, traumatic brain injuries, and post-traumatic stress disorder.

Interacting with animals influences the social interaction between humans and related factors important in this respect, such as trust, empathy, aggression, and a positive mood. A relatively large body of research investigated the effect of a friendly animal on the perception of the human in its company and on the stimulation of social behavior. This is also called the "social catalyst effect" when it refers to the facilitation of interpersonal interactions.

This image is from the Steven Spielberg movie, "The Warhorse." Albert (Jeremy Irvine) and his beloved horse, Joey, live on a farm in the British countryside. At the outbreak of World War I, Albert and Joey are forcibly parted when Albert's father sells the horse to the British cavalry.

Human-Horse Bonding

Human-horse bonding is a two-way street. Animals play interesting roles in our lives just as we do in theirs. How do we account for these emotional relationships?

Does it have to do with the chemicals in our brains? Does it have to do with the nature, quality, and frequency of contact? Does it depend on the extent our senses are activated during each encounter? Is this bonding associated with the time in our lives and their lives? We equestrians do know - it does take place.

My father had a tear in his eye when he parted with his last draft horse. I cried for a week when my first horse, "Duke," was returned to its former owner's pasture to live out his last remaining year.

My day is greatly enhanced, and the stress of the world goes away with a morning drive with four horses under the live oak trees laden with Spanish moss, here in Central Florida.

How Does Bonding Occur?

From "The Horse Connection," Kip Mistral explains it this way: Horses are likely to have what science has identified as a "coherent" heart rhythm" (heart rate pattern), which explains why we may "feel better" when we are around them. Studies have found that a coherent heart pattern or heart rate variability (HRV) is a robust measure of well-being and consistent with emotional states of calm and joy – that is, we exhibit such patterns when we feel positive emotions.

A coherent heart pattern is indicative of a system that can recover and adjust to stressful situations very efficiently. Often, we only need to be in a horse's presence to feel a sense of wellness and peace. Research shows that people experience many physiological benefits while interacting with horses. Lowered blood pressure and heart rate, increased levels of beta-endorphins (neurotransmitters that serve as pain suppressors), decreased stress levels, reduced feelings of anger, hostility, tension and anxiety, improved social functioning; and increased feelings of empowerment, trust, patience, and self-efficacy.

For a horse to pair bond with a human, it must first learn to pair bond with its mother, so that is why we support the development of the mare-foal pair bonding in the critical development phase after birth. After pair bonding with the mother, the foal learns to pair bond with cohorts. Horses that are taught to pair bond by the herd are the horses who subsequently readily pair bond with their human partners and guardians.

To train your horse, pair bond with him, as that is his nature. Bonding requires time and establishment of familiarity. To establish familiarity, spend time with your horse. If you spend all day for days on end with your horse, you will get to know one another deeply, and a true unity can develop. Time is required for bonding - time brushing, rubbing, riding and caring. Show your horse you care for him, and he is likely to pair bond readily.

Bonding is an essential component of domestication. Przewalski's and Zebras are truly wild animals and cannot merge their social structures with humans to be trainable.

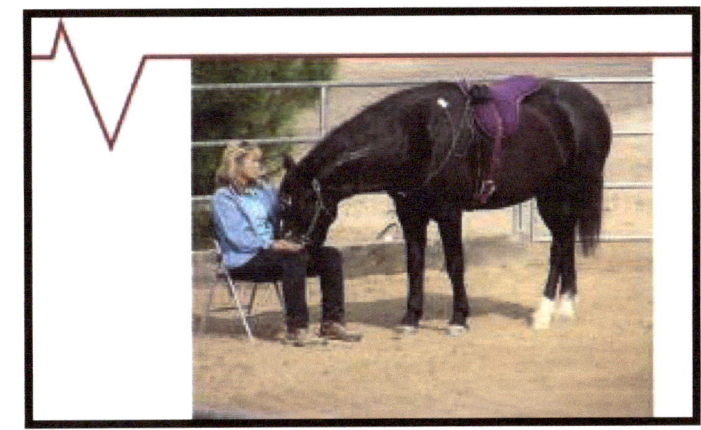

Horses Respond to People

Emotional cues may be carried by humans through different channels: voice (prosody), posture, expression, and pheromones. Horses respond to this element of human presence in their space.

Horses are keenly aware of a person's body language, gestures, and expressions. A person's touch can be kind or menacing. Your voice can reflex your emotions. The smell of your body can be detected by a horse. Many things about you can be detected by the horses. What does this say to us as drivers? If we are nervous, the horse is nervous. When we are calm; the horse is calm.

I know that my horses can read my emotional state. Even when driving four, my feelings are telegraphed through the reins, my voice, and mere presence.

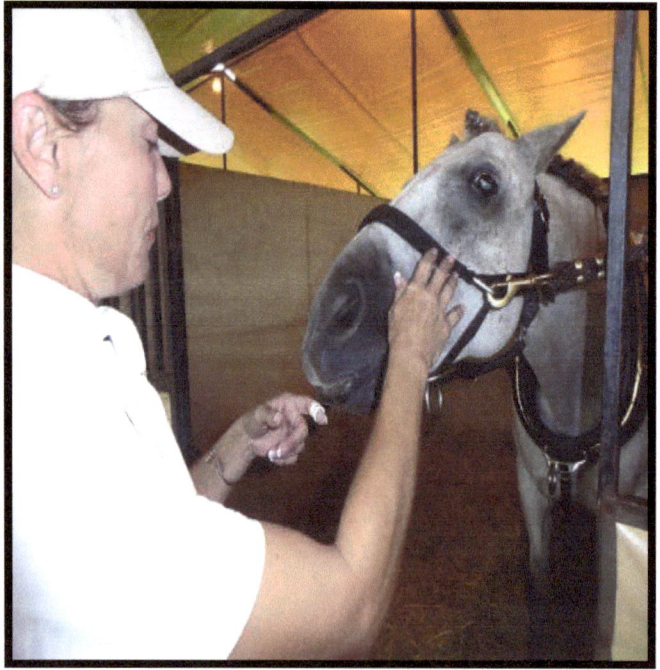

Horses Can Read Human Emotions

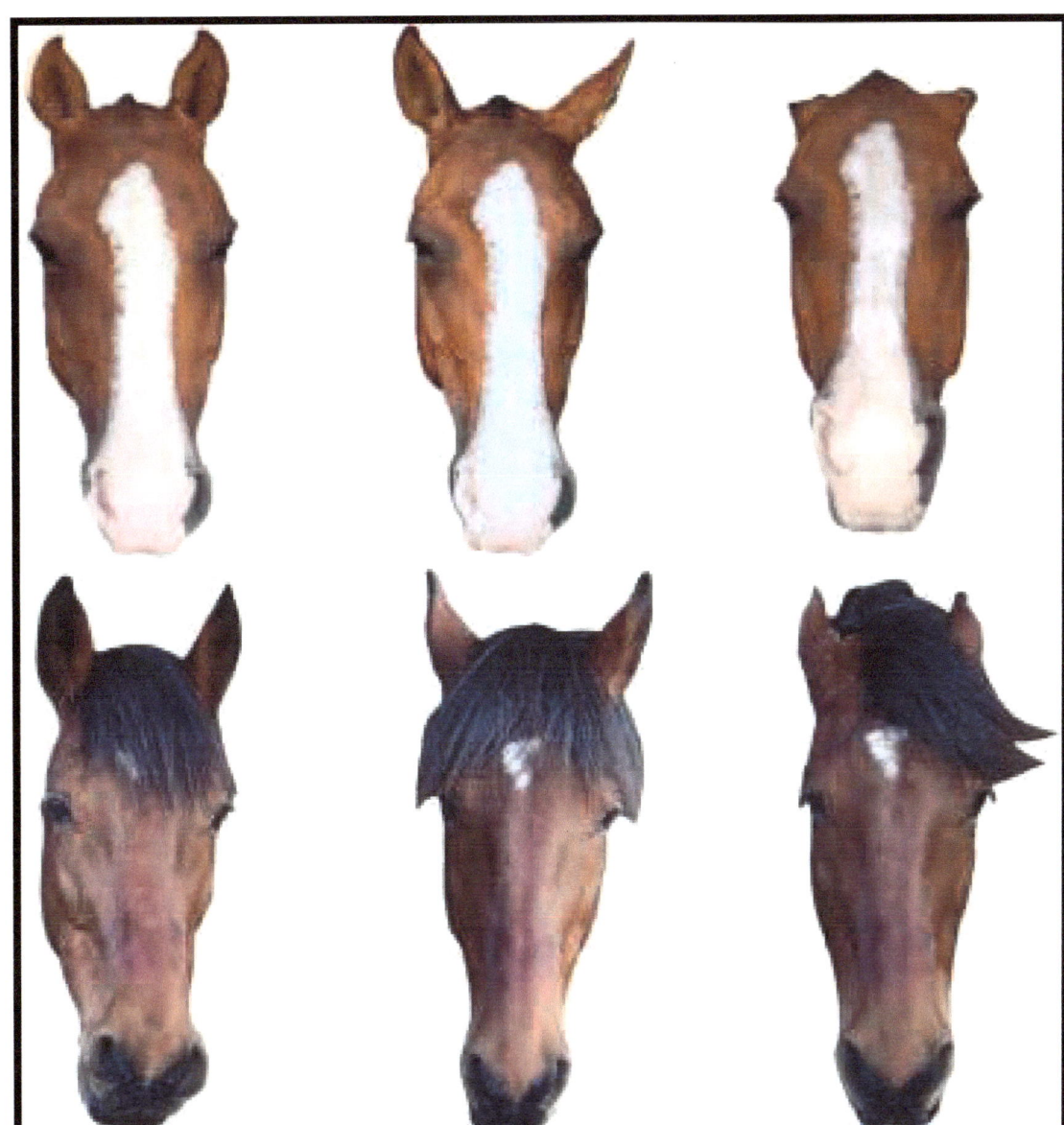

Scientists at the University of Sussex near Brighton in England have compiled a directory of facial expressions in one of humanity's oldest four-legged friends. Their Equine Facial Action Coding System (EquiFACS for short) has identified 17 discrete facial movements in horses that may indicate mood, intention or just bafflement. This is at least three more than the facial expressions identified in chimpanzees. Dogs can get a message across with 16 different expressions. Human faces have 27 different ways of speaking silently, with the lips and eyes and the occasional wrinkled nose.

The horses were recruited from five riding or livery stables in Sussex and Surrey, UK, between April 2014 and February 2015. They were shown happy and angry photographs of two unfamiliar male faces. The experimental tests examined the horses' spontaneous reactions to the photos, with no prior training, and the experimenters were not able to see which photographs they were displayed so they could not inadvertently influence the horses.

"Horses are predominantly visual animals, with eyesight that's better than domestic cats and dogs, yet their use of facial expressions has been largely overlooked. What surprised us was the rich repertoire of complex facial movements in horses, and how many of them are similar to humans," said Jennifer Waltham, a doctoral researcher and one of the lead authors.

"Despite the differences in facial structure between horses and humans, we were able to identify some similar expressions about movements of lips and eyes. What we'll now be looking at is how these expressions relate to emotional states."

Sussex psychologists studied how 28 horses reacted to seeing photographs of positive versus negative human facial expressions. When viewing angry faces, horses looked more with their left eye, a behavior associated with perceiving negative stimuli. The horse's reactions included heart rate increase and more stress-related behaviors.

The study, published in "Biology Letters," concludes that this response indicates that the horses had a functionally relevant understanding of the angry faces they were seeing. The effect of facial expressions on heart rate has not been seen before in interactions between animals and humans.

Amy Smith, a doctoral student in the Mammal Vocal Communication and Cognition Research Group at Sussex, co-led the research. She said: "What's interesting about this research is that it shows that horses can read emotions across the species barrier. We have known for a long time that horses are a socially sophisticated species, but this is the first time we have seen that they can distinguish between positive and negative human facial expressions.

"The reaction to the angry facial expressions was particularly clear–there was a quicker increase in their heart rate, and the horses moved their heads to look at the angry faces with their left eye."

Research shows that many species view negative events with their left eye due to the right brain hemisphere's specialization for processing threatening stimuli (information from the left eye is processed in the right hemisphere).

Amy continued: "It's interesting to note that the horses had a strong reaction to the negative expressions, but less so to the positive. This may be because it is particularly important for animals to recognize threats in their environment. In this context, recognizing angry faces may act as a warning system, allowing horses to anticipate negative human behavior such as rough handling."

A tendency for viewing negative human facial expressions with the left eye has also been documented in dogs.

Professor Karen McComb, a co-lead author of the research, said: "There are several possible explanations for our findings. Horses may have adapted an ancestral ability for reading emotional cues in other horses to respond appropriately to human facial expressions during their co-evolution.

"Alternatively, individual horses may have learned to interpret human expressions during their lifetime. What's interesting is that accurate assessment of negative emotions is possible across the species barrier despite the dramatic difference in facial morphology between horses and humans."

"Emotional awareness is likely to be very important in highly social species like horses–and our ongoing research is examining the relationship between a range of emotional skills and social behavior."

Amy Smith and Professor McComb are based in the School of Psychology at Sussex. The study is co-authored by Sussex colleagues Dr. Leanne Proops, Kate Grounds and Dr. Jennifer Wathan. This research is part of an ongoing project into emotional awareness in horses that is funded by the Leverhulme Trust and the University of Sussex.

From "Horses Discriminate Between Facial Expressions of Conspecifics" J. Wathan, L. Proops, K. Grounds & K. McComb Scientific Reports 6, Article number: 38322 (2016) doi:10.1038/srep38322

The British Queens and Horses

The Queen and Queen Mother have long loved their horses. The Royal household keeps stables of riding and carriage horses. From an early age, Queen Elizabeth II has had a keen interest in horses of all kinds. Throughout her reign, this has developed into one of her main leisure time activities, and she takes great pride in her "home bred" horses, including her interest in breeding thoroughbreds for racing. As well as thoroughbreds, Queen Elizabeth also breeds Shetland ponies at Balmoral in Scotland and Fell ponies at Hampton Court. In 2007 she opened a full—time Highland pony stud at Balmoral to enhance and preserve the breed.

Horses and People with Special Needs

Equestrian therapy (also known as equine therapy or Equine-Assisted Therapy [EAT]) or Hippotherapy) is a form of therapy that makes use of horses to help promote emotional growth. Equestrian therapy is particularly applied to patients with ADD, anxiety, autism, dementia, delay in mental development, Down Syndrome and other genetic syndromes, depression, trauma and brain injuries, behavior and abuse issues and other mental health issues.

Autism is now classified as an epidemic in the CDC, estimating 1 in 68 children are identified with autism spectrum disorder. It is five times more common in male children. The Autism spectrum disorder foundation in 2016 stated: "Equine therapy is highly beneficial to children with autism. It helps them develop their core skills more naturally, skills they need to function in society."

There are other problems such as endocrine disruption, cancer, and obesity that affects 30% of the US population in which association with this large animal has proven to be effective.

Association with horses has also been proven effective in helping those with post-traumatic stress disorder and limited mobility.

The basis of the therapy is that horses behave similarly to human beings in their social and responsive behavior, it is easy for patients to establish a connection with the horse. Please research Equestrian Therapy to learn more.

The pictures at the right are those taken when I was operating, what is now called, The Grand Oaks Resort. I sponsored an annual regional horse show for special needs riders and a program for persons who used wheelchairs including veterans.

What about the Brain Chemicals?

Can the association with the horse naturally produce these chemicals in the brain?

- Endocannabinoids: "The Bliss Molecule"
- Dopamine: "The Reward Molecule"
- Oxytocin: "The Bonding Molecule"
- Endorphin: "The Pain-Killing Molecule"
- GABA: "The Anti-Anxiety Molecule"
- Serotonin: "The Confidence Molecule"
- Adrenaline: "The Energy Molecule"
- Noradrenaline: "The Fight-or-flight Mechanism Molecule"

These neurotransmitters in the brain may affect the way we feel about our animals or even how our animals feel about us.

"Evidence-Based Horsemanship" was developed out of a collaboration between renowned horseman, Martin Black, and neuroscientist, Dr. Stephen Peters who felt that the public and their horses needed a source of "real information" gathered by observation, tested in the field and validated by science."

Some believe in the spirituality of this horse-human relationship. More and more people are seeking verification of what they know or feel happening to themselves and their horses as they relate to one another.

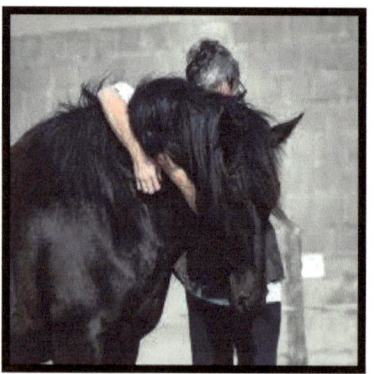

Oxytocin

Is there oxytocin, the bonding chemical, in the horse-human relationship?

My answer to this question is–yes.

Oxytocin is a hormone secreted by the pituitary gland and stored in the brain. It is the drug of touch. This chemical in our brains can break-down social barriers, induce feelings of optimism, increase self-esteem, read the body language of others, and build trust. It decreases anxiety and makes us calm.

Can it help with post-traumatic stress syndrome?

Can it help children and adults with autism?

Can you get it from touching horses?

iBrain Technology

iBrain is the world's first portable brain scanner to help research psychiatric drugs and assist in understanding neurological diseases. NeuroVigil, the company that developed iBrain, has now partnered with a large pharmaceutical company which plans to deploy the iBrain technology in its pharmaceutical research. Can this portable scanner help in identifying the chemicals in our brains that come naturally through our association with the horse?

The iBrain is a portable and user-friendly single-channel EEG recording device. An electroencephalogram (EEG) is a test used to evaluate the electrical activity in the brain. Brain cells communicate with each other through electrical impulses. An EEG can be used to help detect normality or potential problems associated with this activity.

What goes on when horse people feel great pleasure in the company of our horses, or the joy of getting them to perform, or even experience pleasure looking at pictures of horses?

Can we examine the activity in the horse's brain through its association with us?

What does the horse seem to need in this relationship that seems to produce the desired level of communication for performance?

Visualization

Training the mind is training the body! Mental training is critical to achievement in an athletic or physically based skill like carriage driving. Mental exercise can improve almost all of our abilities and fast-track us towards our goals. Visualization can help in all sorts of activities. Relaxation and visualization, as it relates to the movement of the body, seem to be the keys to successful performance. It can also help you to capture the feeling of being physically active, and of being a winner. Relaxation and visualization are helpful to a carriage driver because you can devote your brain power to the activity of racing through a cones course or a forest or carefully executing a dressage test.

Practice by itself does not make perfect. Perfect practice makes perfect! This is why you have to understand communicating with your driving horse, and proper use of the aids before the desired result can be practiced over and over again to be successful.

I often talk about happy, relaxed horses. Well, we need a happy and relaxed driver. Nervousness and stress radically reduce one's ability to learn, visualize, and perform. Think it and feel it. Visualize already being the champion and how that might feel.

I train my horses in the same harness and carriage that I use at an event. I also try to dress as I would at an event. I even wear the same gloves so that I might visualize and feel the way it will be at an event.

Imagine yourself a winner, focus on the positive and the good feelings. Get the picture and feeling of the lateral movements needed when in the corners of the dressage ring or driving around the stone pillars at a manor house.

Developing skills to drive requires acquiring skills and getting progressively better and building confidence. Think yourself a winner.

Establish a Goal and Set a Plan

You must set a goal that motivates you and is realistic based on your time and resources. You cannot be world champion without the time and resources to do so. Remember to balance your life so the ups and downs in one segment of your life, don't get you down in another. Achievement of one's goals requires commitment.

Make sure the goal is yours, not what others want for you. Take small steps and reset your goals so you can account for your accomplishments along the way. Goals have to be clear and well defined. Remember, as you achieve your goals, they will evolve, so be prepared to review and adjust your plans as need be.

After I won two championships with a pair of horses, I started thinking "what next?" I questioned whether I would drive four horses or drive my single horse more in Combined Driving Events (CDE) which I had done successfully at the first Live Oak CDEs. Fortunately, I had the time and the resources to move to driving four to a big coach like Jack Pemberton, so I chose that route. My goals were realized when I won the North American titles of Four-in-hand Champion and Coaching Champion in 1998.

To accomplish goals, you have to stick with it or modify your direction based on circumstances and based on the changes that life just throws at you. Modification of your planning can often offer new and wonderful opportunities. Age is a factor in my planning now. This modification has just opened new pathways for goal setting where I can still keep driving.

I like a GPS.

Keeping Your Focus

For those of us that are easily distracted by others and the surrounding activity, keeping our attention and focus on the task at hand is difficult. We have to remind ourselves to stay focused constantly. Don't let up until the activity is over. For me, that is when the horses are back to the stable, tent or trailer and unhitched.

Don't let others distract you when walking the cones course.

Some get distracted by their mistakes. Recovery counts. Carry on and get back on task as quickly as possible and act as if nothing happened. So, you hit a cone, or your horse didn't bend correctly chin up and keep going.

<u>Do not focus on other's mistakes longer than to learn what went wrong. Do not dwell on the negative. Do not keep images of accidents in your mind. Dwell only on the positive and things with positive outcomes.</u>

You must keep in mind that you must go past the finish line. Often people let up their focus and energy before the end of the dressage test because they are excited that they have done a good job or they see the end in sight–well don't. It is not over until it is over. And that means you need to be out of the view of the judges and back at the stable safely.

Some people take focus boosting breaks which means they breathe deeply and stop, look, listen and smell their environment and then refocus on the task of memorizing the cones course or dressage test.

Being organized, eating properly and drinking enough water all help to improve outcomes. Routine to your day, week, and driving workout all help the performance. My granddaughter has a routine each time she serves a volleyball. I have a routine for warming up and exercising horses. The carriage driver has to have a routine just as his or her horse needs a routine.

Work to Acquire Unconscious Competence

Unconscious competence is sometimes called muscle memory. It is the state where we can drive our horses and talk at the same time without losing focus on the horse's body language and the activity we are performing. Unconscious competence requires repetition and practical training to acquire.

This model suggests there are four stages needed to drive with competence. We first are unaware of our inability to do something. We then become aware of what we don't know. We then know how to do it, but it takes great effort and then we finally can perform a task like it is second nature to us.

Initially described as "Four Stages of Learning Any New Skill," the theory was developed at Gordon Training International, by its employee Noel Burch in the 1970s:

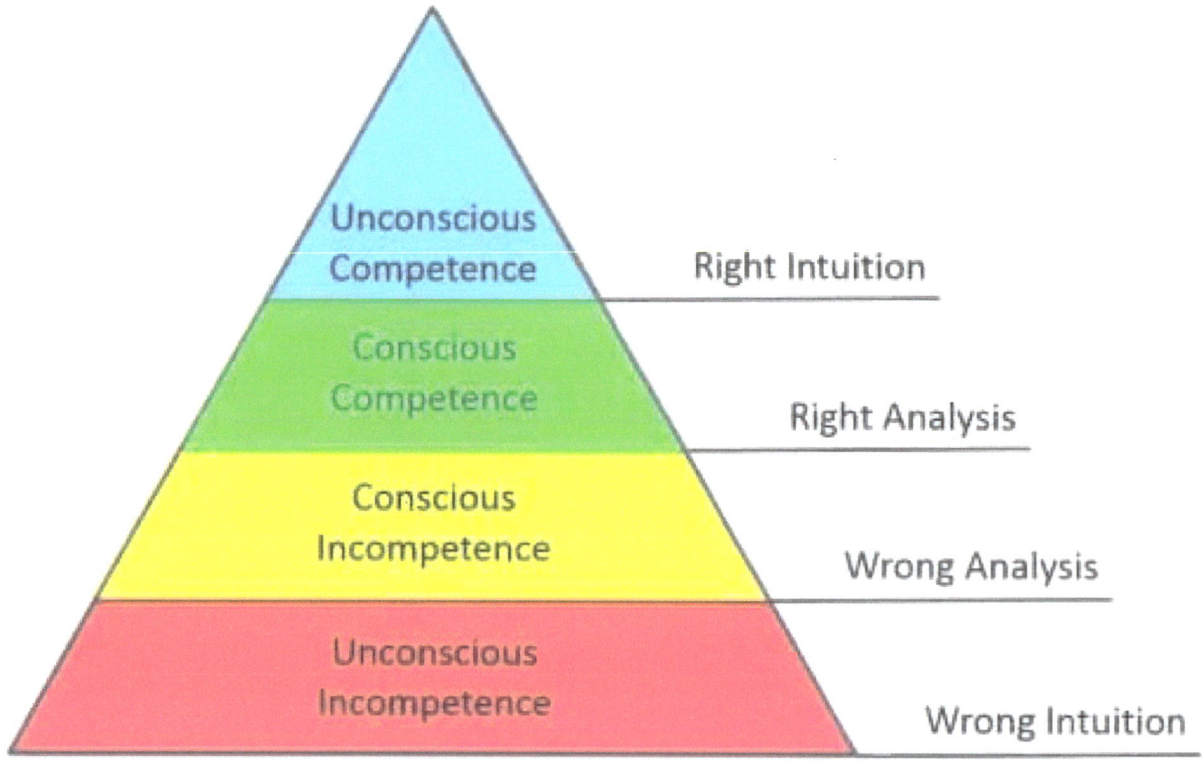

Handling Stress

Deep breathing techniques are helpful in all areas of your life, not just competitive situations. This is currently called square breathing. This can be easily done on the box seat while waiting for your turn in the arena or on the course.

Sensing muscle tension, which is a sign of stress, can prompt you to focus on relaxing the muscles in the lower back which seems to be of particular concern to carriage drivers. The need for proper body posture when driving is key to communicating with the horse. The horse can distinguish subtle differences.

Realistic mental rehearsals of the cones course or hazards and review of anticipated problem situations can be helpful in the proper execution of the tasks approaching.

You may have to find a technique that works for you. Sometimes mental and physical disengagement from circumstances is helpful to relieve stress. But sometimes engagement or psyching oneself works and then building stress for a good performance is helpful.

Positive self-talk or imaging of your past successes can help prepare you for the task ahead.

Imaging and mimicking behavior of other successful competitors can solicit the behavior needed to execute a task successfully.

Many use support team distractions by either engaging or blocking individuals. Conversational distractions are sometimes helpful. I often like to have people around me who are good conversationalists, which keeps me in a state of relaxation. Smiling is very helpful. It conveys an air of confidence to the judge and is also helpful with relaxation by the release of endorphins in the brain

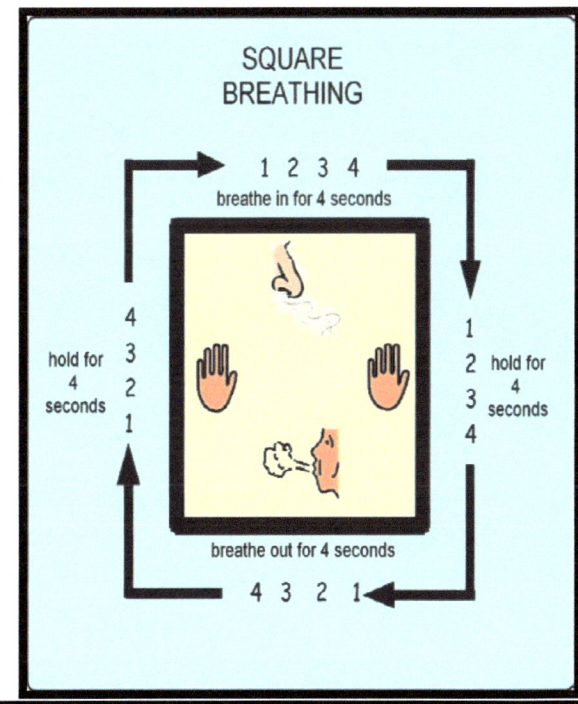

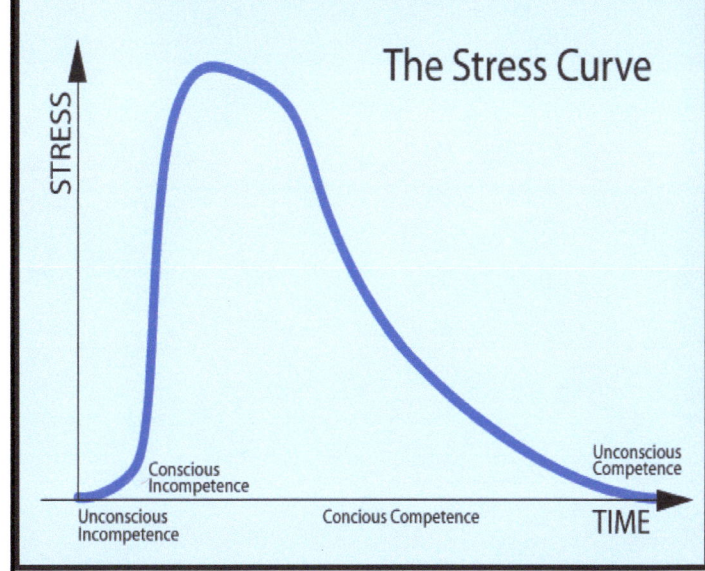

TALKING WITH A HORSE

Establish Yourself as the Leader

David Lewis gives a good explanation of getting respect from your horse.

"Establishing yourself as the leader will cause your horse to respect you. He will begin to lose his aggressiveness toward you if he respects you as his leader.

When developing your relationship with your horse, always be firm and gentle. Don't let the horse disrespect you. When you are feeding or grooming him, don't let him rub on you. This is a sign of disrespect. The rule of thumb is that you can enter into the horse's space, but he is never allowed to come into your space without being invited. Your space is your personal "bubble." When he shows you a sign of disrespect or enters your space, make him hustle his feet backward. Do whatever is necessary to get your horse out of your space. For all new horses, I always carry a training stick that allows me to move their feet and get them out of my space without allowing them to get too close.

The first step in establishing yourself as a leader is gaining your horse's respect and trust. Horses establish respect by movement, either causing their feet to move or inhibiting movement. The first rule in horsemanship is: whoever moves first loses. If you don't make your horse move his feet forwards, backward, left and right and you don't maintain that respect between the two of you, his behavior will get worse. Horses are extremely smart and learn quickly.

You have to prove to your horse that you are worthy of the leadership role. You do this by moving his feet forwards, backward, left and right and always rewarding the slightest try. When the leader of the herd tells the other horses to move, they better move, or he's going to back it up with action. He'll kick, bite and do whatever it takes to get the other horse's feet to move. The more you can move your horse's feet, and the less you move your own, the more effective leader you will become and the greater control you will have. The less you can move your horse's feet, the less control you will have, and your horse will become more disrespectful.

Establishing yourself as a better leader and getting greater respect from your horse will translate to your horse becoming more respectful around other people as well."

The picture is of Chris Irwin in *California Riding Magazine* in the article "The Power of Why Frame of Body = Frame of Mind."

Foal Imprinting

Foal imprinting, popularized by Dr. Robert Miller, is an early way to develop bonding with humans. Early handling of the foal by a person makes later training much easier. If the young horse becomes familiar with the smell, voice, and touch of a human through gentle means, it is the start of the mental processes that are keys to developing trust later in the horse's life.

This is an overview of Dr. Miller's imprint training of a foal:

Bonding with the imprint trainer: Immediately postpartum, the foal bonds simultaneously with its dam and with one or more persons handling it. Such foals see humans, not as predators, but as fellow horses.

Submission, but not fear: During imprint training, the foal cannot escape (its natural method of survival) exposure to frightening stimuli. As a result, it becomes dependent and submissive in its attitude. The foal sees the trainer as a dominant horse or herd leader. Psychologically, this is the ideal relationship between horse and human. We must have submissiveness in a horse if he is to work for us. But, the submissiveness should be created not by fear (a predatory role) but by dependence (a dominant leader role).

Desensitization to most sensory stimuli (visual, auditory, tactile, and olfactory): Most parts of the body, including all body openings, are desensitized. Rapid, repetitious stimuli (flooding) are used until the foal is habituated, i.e., permanently non-responsive to those stimuli. Loud noises, fluttering objects or being touched anywhere on the body will after that be calmly tolerated.

Sensitizing to performance related stimuli: Specifically, the foal can be taught to respond (rather than habituated) to head and flank pressure. The responsiveness allows control over the fore and hindquarters. The foal will lead where directed and will move its hind end laterally in response to the touch of a finger in the flank region. This is best taught on the day after birth after the foal is on its feet." From www.robertmmiller.com.

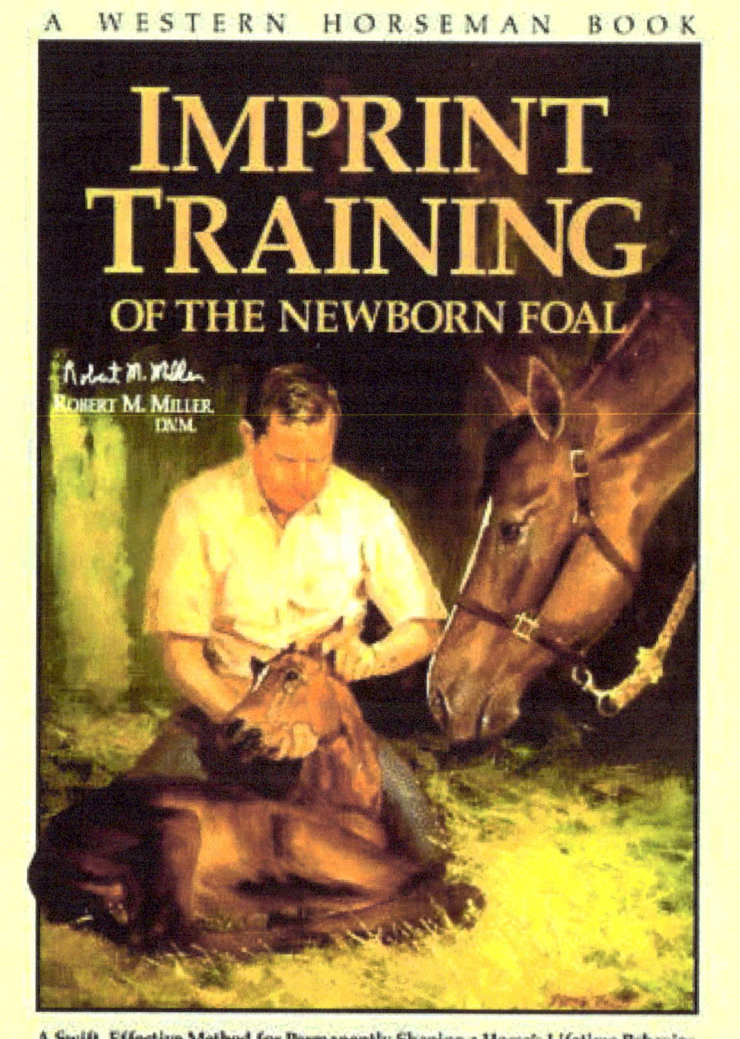

Training the Person

Training the person (you) may take more effort than training the horse. Forgive the pun again, but a "stable" person leads to a "stable" horse.

Keeping a calm and cool demeanor is essential when working with horses. Horses can sense your nervousness and anxiety, never allow yourself to get angry. Just try a different approach or different method to communicate with your horse.

Work with and observe professionals that are masters and teachers in the particular disciple in which you are interested. Some people can do and not teach others. Listen to the successful teachers and observe the successful doers.

Building a skill level to hold and manipulate the reins and whip is essential. The use of a rein board is good for learning the principles, but the only way you can learn your reinsmanship is to practice with a horse.

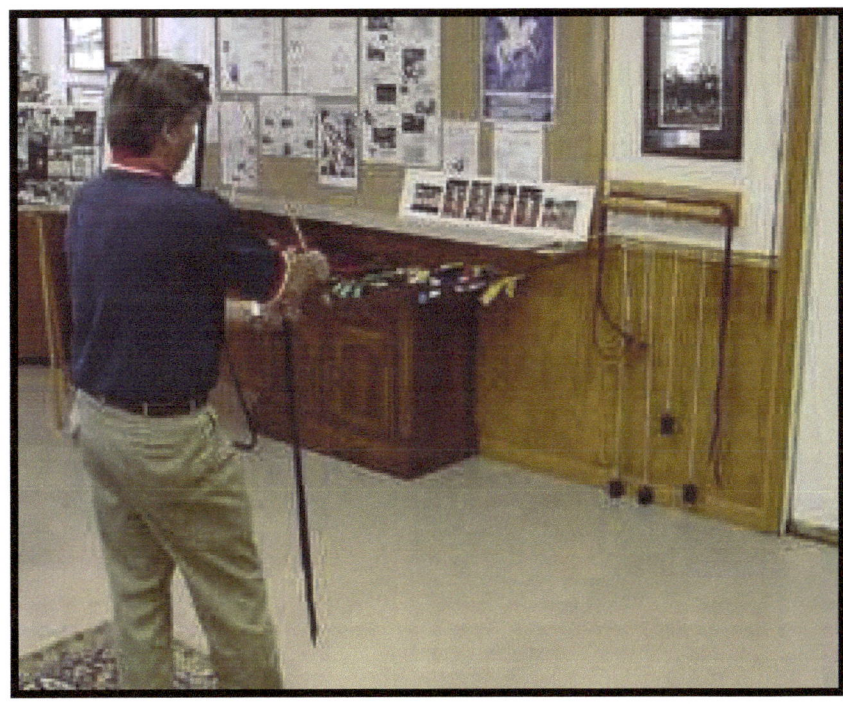

I recommend, particularly for women, who are 50% less strong in our upper bodies, the use of weights and squeeze balls to build strength particularly as you progress to driving four horses.

Role models are very helpful. Select some people who are already successful drivers and try to emulate their demeanor and style. Take lessons with an experienced driving horse with a reputable professional.

There is no substitute for practice or repetition - so drive, drive, drive. Athletes, surgeons, and ballroom dancers do not get good without repetition, repetition, repetition.

Training Principles

Don't rush the training of a young horse or an older saddle horse that is learning to drive.

There is no place for anger when teaching a horse to drive. If a particular system does not work, it is up to the creative trainer to come up with a new method.

The early steps of training the horse are to stand quietly when tied, lead, and load. With driving horses, we coordinate the decided action with a voice command. For instance, we say the word "back" with whatever visual or tactile command used to get the horse to back when led by a halter and lead line. Much can be done with the horse in halter in an enclosed space when training. One can make even a long line or drive from the ground with the horse in just a halter and two long lunge lines. Once bitted, the horse can be ground driven with typical reins like in the pictures below.

When training your horse, make sure the horse walks first and takes the inside and outside rein from the ground. Always make sure the horse can halt and stand quietly without sight of its handler. It may be necessary to start with a header, but make sure the horse is comfortable standing without a header.

For the driving horse, it is important that training should concentrate on the walk and halt, walk and halt, walk and halt, so the horse thoroughly understands the word "whoa."

Training can then move to more of the trot and walk, again, making sure the horse understands the halt. When the horse is ready and thoroughly understands the prior step, trainers can introduce something new, but they end their session with what is familiar to the horse so to end with a positive exercise

Tips for Training the Horse

I recommend developing consistent procedures when training your horse. Try to do things, in the same way, every day. Drive at the same time each day. Use the same techniques to catch and lead the horse. Take the horse to the same "home base" to cross tie and groom. Use the same people to handle the horse. These routines are essential underpinnings for the horse and human to develop good habits that get built into our unconscious memories.

Horse's learn to tolerate irrelevant circumstances. By habituating to less important signals, an animal can focus its attention on the most important features of its environment.

Keep sessions to the horse's conditioning and mental tolerance level. Horses can work for longer and longer periods of time with little adverse effects providing its feed is commensurate to the exertion.

Each session should consist of reviewing things already learned, the introduction of some new things and then going back to that which is already done well.

Every time you interact with your horse you are teaching him something whether you intend to or not

We always include standing still (usually while chatting with a friend) and one rein back in each session.

Adding weight to your carriage can build your horses tolerance for large coaches. This can be done by just adding additional people on your outings with an everyday carriage.

I always recommend training in the type of harness (full collar and breast collar) you are going to use for your driving.

Bonding and Grooming

Bonding and good communication depend on timing, consistency, and repetition and a calm, even demeanor. The brain chemistry of both the horse and human are altered through proximity and touching. This is just another reason why the grooming and ground care of the horse are important.

These are images of quiet, relaxed horses that are cross-tied at their usual location for grooming and harnessing. Just like our home and family offer stability and routine to our lives, so do the stable and this "home base" for the horse. This is where the gentle brushing and care takes place. This should be a daily activity. This routine offers stability so the horse can venture forth into the world.

Please refer to "Basic Horse Safety Manuals," such as the one from the University of Kentucky or American Youth Horse Council for some of the best practices around horses.

Observers of Body Language

The start of the driver's training is to become a keen observer of the body language since the horse cannot speak and tell us what it is thinking. The best of horse whisperers and natural horsemanship trainers throughout history have been gifted in "reading the horse" and not thinking that all horses are alike. There may be different strategies that work at differing times in the horse's training. There are no hard and fast rules, and "timing" is everything.

John Lyons, known as "America's Most Trusted Horseman," has developed a system of directing the horse in a round pen through his ability to read and respond to the character and body language of the horse. He is skilled at timing his cues (his body and hand movements) based on the horse's body language and temperament. John depends on the horse's vision to respond to his cues.

Good horse trainers are:
- Keen observers and are great at timing and application.
- Patient and know the value of repetition.
- Disciplined in their daily routine.
- Problem solvers, in that - if one thing does not work, try another.
- Knowledgeable about horses and their behavior.
- Understanding of the stress the horse is under learning new things.
- Excellent communicators know how to push the horse's buttons too.

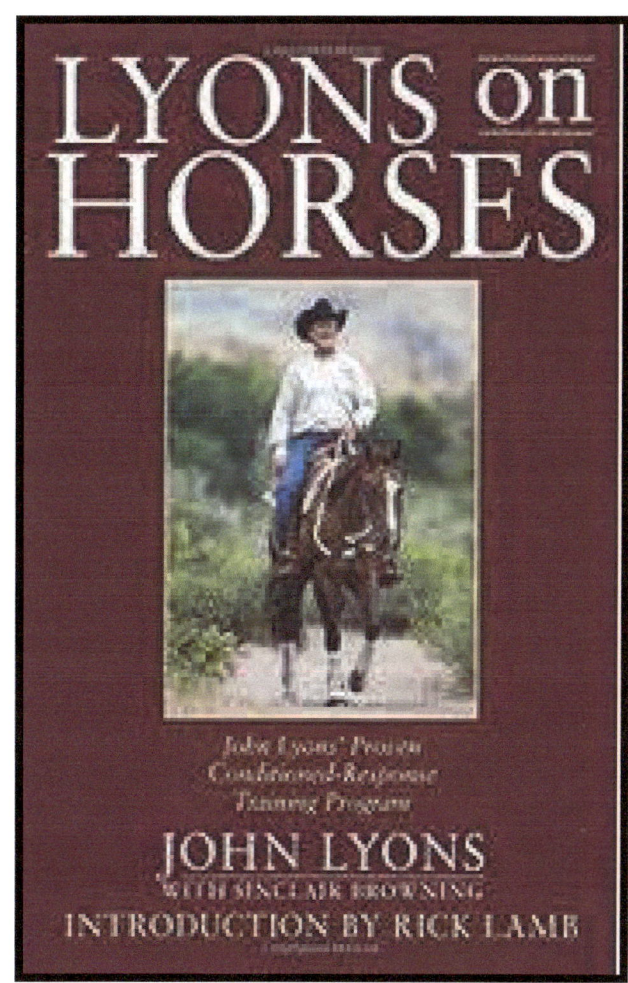

Overcoming Fear

We want the horse to remain calm, overcome its fears, listen, and respond to the direction of the rider or carriage driver. When frightened, they run like these horses in the top picture.

When trained and accustomed to human hostlers, they stay relaxed and quiet as they appear in the second picture of me at the Royal Mews preparing for the British Driving Society's Sunday drive on the grounds of Windsor Castle in 1999. We were invited to stay here at the Queen's stable.

The bottom picture shows the training of mounted police horses going through some extensive training to overcome their fears of all sorts of obstacles and hazards. The process of continued exposure to objects that are viewed as scary is the key of well-behaved horses. By circling closer and closer to the scary object or passing back and forth or over and over the object of fear, it can teach the horse that it is not going to hurt nor cause pain.

Scary Things

There are various ways to help a horse to overcome unwanted shying at flower pots or puddles. Some persons believe in gradual exposure and asking the horse to move little by little up to the scary thing and putting its muzzle on the object. This may work well for some saddle horses, but is not so easily done with a horse and a carriage. If they startle and back up quickly, they can capsize a carriage.

I find that circling in one direction and then another near the scary thing works best. The driver can get progressively closer with each pass. This exposure without touching it or getting hurt can help the horse not to fear certain sights or sounds. This circling by the object in both directions is necessary because of the horse's monocular and binocular vision. It must be exposed to the unfamiliar from both sides.

Stop passing the scary thing when you are satisfied there is just a look or a slight deviation. Remember to never get into a fight with your horse. Do the best you can but don't insist on too much at one time. Over time the horse will trust your judgment about scary things.

Again, it is beneficial to work a less experienced horse in a pair with a senior experienced horse. The confidence of the older horse does wonders in helping the young horse to overcome extreme reaction to fearful things.

Each horse is an individual, some horses shy, some bolt, some stop and freeze in place. I prefer the horse that stops and doesn't overreact.

Consistent Persistence

Even though horses are called domesticated, they are not like other animals because of their size, strength, and speed–the factors that made them valuable to man throughout history. Once in the hands of man and trained, horses were used for warfare, transportation, commerce, trade, agriculture, and industry. To be useful, humanity had to understand what the horse needed and still get our needs met.

The building of trust is paramount in training and communicating with horses. When the horse is consistently treated with kindness and not abused or physically harmed, the horse will trust the human.

Trust can only be built through contact and use. Horses that work seem to be happier and have less anxiety than horses that are left wild. They seem to take comfort in learning the world of humans. Horses need consistent human handling and daily work. It is best to have the same people work around your horse, so the horse can recognize and trust the person will not hurt or abuse them. These handlers are traditionally called "hostlers."

I believe that equine behavior is influenced by the personality and emotional state of this handler, so it is important to have a non-threatening, calm, confident hostlers.

These people need to be consistent in their communication and then use the same methods consistently. Since voice is one of the aids for driving, I recommend the use of the voice when working around horses. Be consistent with your language; this is vital in training. If you encourage the horse to walk, use the command "walk." When halting the horse at a cross-tie area, use the term "whoa."

Repetition, repetition, and more repetition of the works and actions and activities, the better it is for the horse to understand.

Nagging is Legitimate

Years ago, an old or worn-out horse might be called a "nag," which is a term from the old Dutch for a small saddle horse. The men who worked with these old nag horses were often called "naggers." The term is also found in old Swedish to mean to complain or to bite or gnaw.

Believe it or not, nagging is a legitimate form of horse training. We ask, ask, ask and when the horse responds we stop. So we become naggers just as we do with our household partners by saying, "Take the garbage out." "Take the garbage out." "Take the garbage out." When our partner does it, we stop our nagging.

We signal the horse until the horse responds and then we stop the pressure or the tapping. So, I annoy by constant urging, stop when receiving the correct response.

Gordon Wright called this a system of reward and punishment. "Punishment is not necessarily the application of spur or whip to his sides. The reward is a lack of punishment. When the rider's legs close against his horse, asking him to move forward, that is punishment. When the horse obeys that command, the legs relax. That is his reward…"

Xenophon also talked about their being no need for harsh treatment and the need for reward.

I like to call this system nagging. We apply pressure to ask, and the release of pressure is the reward. It does not mean to let go completely such as in the use of the reins. It just means to stop nagging.

The same is true for loading a horse in the trailer: tap, tap, tap the horse on the hip and when he steps forward - stop - and then repeat.

Voice Intonations

Intonation is as important if not more so than the words you use. A soothing voice can be used for downward transitions whereas a brisk sharper intonation is used for upward transitions.

I often praise a horse in a comforting voice and often let the horse know when it is focusing on something it might perceive as scary that I see it and I will say, in a comforting voice, "It is ok, I see it."

Sometimes I use a louder more forceful voice if I think the horse is going to shy at something to convey that he has more to fear from me than the scary object.

Examples of Voice Commands

Preparation Commands	Commands	Impulsion	Turns	Transitions
Heads Up	Whoa	Kissing (Impulsion)	Gee and Haw	Easy Up and Walk
"horse's name"	Walk	Clucking (Cadence)	Come and Get	OK and Whoa
A-n-d	Trot	Swishing (extension)	Left and Right	Heads Up, Trot
Easy Up	Canter	Whistle (canter)		

Voice and Multiples

When driving multiples, there are few additional things to consider when using the voice.

- 🐎 Horses need to work together, so preparation commands become more important to coordinate.
- 🐎 Each horse should know their name.
- 🐎 Names should be distinct and not like commands or other horse's names.
- 🐎 Transitions take longer with more horses.
- 🐎 Change the position of a horse or substitute a horse of one less capable.

Repeat…. Repeat…. Repeat….

Keep a daily routine of handling and work. This is a practice that fosters good communication that develops into trust.

The elder coachman who was always asked how to solve a particular problem with a particular horse always responded: "Drive him 20 miles." That was the old man's wisdom. Just work the horse and spend time with the horse and he will learn to be your horse and to respond to your requests.

Those who get the best performance from their horse spend hours and hours with their animal. Training for optimal performance takes time. It takes an hour of work on the part of the rider or driver.

These trainer and armature drivers must be consistent in the use of their communication cues, but they understand that each horse is different. Therefore, they adapt their responses according to the personality of each horse. Some horses are lazy or need more encouragement and others require less. Know your horse and know what works for each horse. The amount of reassurance varies from horse to horse.

The name of the game is "Repeat, Repeat, and Repeat." Learning takes time. Just like humans who perform any skill set, repetition is important. Ballroom dancers, ballerinas, and carriage drivers only learn their craft through practice, practice, practice.

Progressive Conditioning

Gradually build for distance travel according to your upcoming events. Heart monitors are helpful, but observing manual readings and observation can also be skillfully used.

Interval training is a label often associated with gradually increasing stress and exercise levels.

At heart rates of 140 beats per minute [bpm] or below, the horse's respiratory system is said to be functioning aerobically, with the blood supplying oxygen to the cells, including the muscle cells. The horse can continue working at this pace for long periods without fatigue.

However, when the heart rate reaches 150-160 bpm and above (during a very fast canter), lactic acid is released into the muscles and the horse tires. Any further increase in speed or effort results in the production of more lactic acid; this is described as the anaerobic phase.

Anaerobic exercise cannot be sustained for long periods, but as the horse becomes fitter, his aerobic capacity will increase, the anaerobic phase will be delayed, and his recovery rates, overall fitness, and stamina will improve.

The reason the carriage driving horse can sustain the trot for a long period when conditioned properly is the horse seldom reaches the anaerobic stage at the trot.

Learn to take your horse's TPRs–temperature, pulse, and respiration to learn your horse's reading at rest and consult your veterinarian for limits for your type of endeavor. There are monitors available to use while your horse in on-the-move. It is interesting to see variations in heart rate on differing terrain, in and out of shape, and up and down hills. All of these activities can build the proper muscling including the heart.

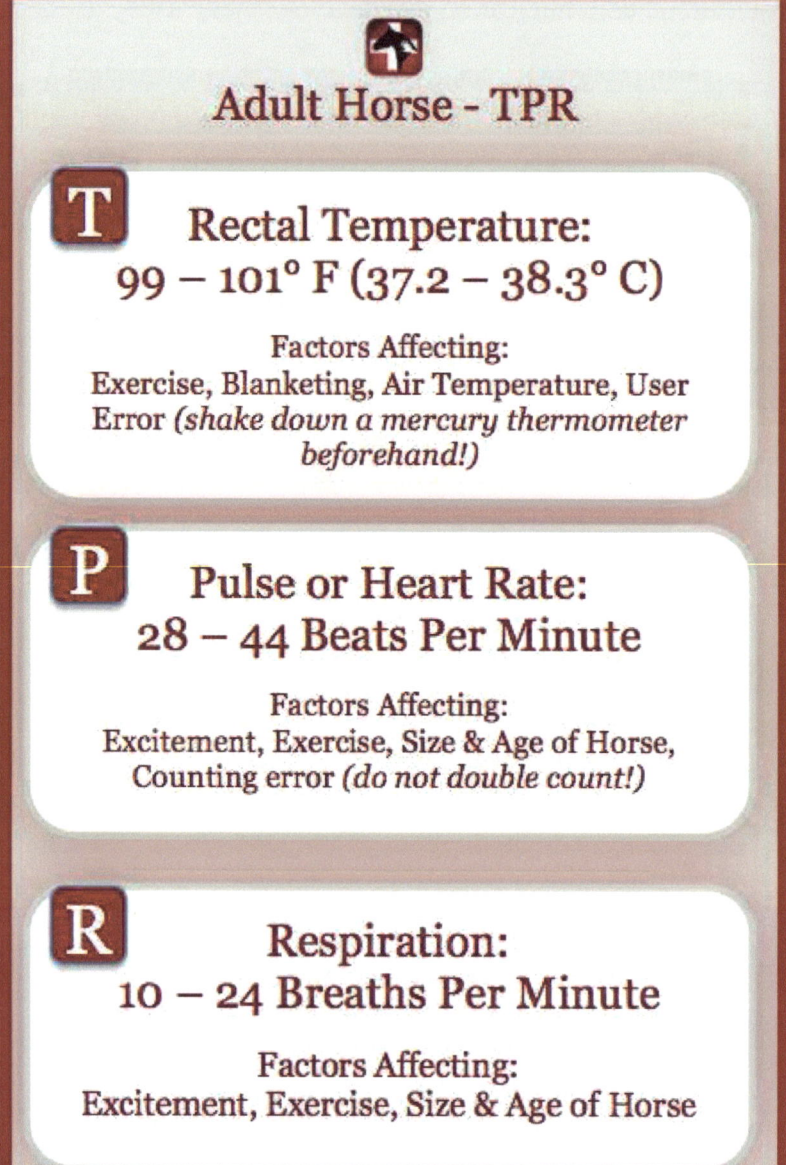

Adult Horse - TPR

T **Rectal Temperature:**
99 – 101° F (37.2 – 38.3° C)

Factors Affecting:
Exercise, Blanketing, Air Temperature, User Error *(shake down a mercury thermometer beforehand!)*

P **Pulse or Heart Rate:**
28 – 44 Beats Per Minute

Factors Affecting:
Excitement, Exercise, Size & Age of Horse, Counting error *(do not double count!)*

R **Respiration:**
10 – 24 Breaths Per Minute

Factors Affecting:
Excitement, Exercise, Size & Age of Horse

Health Inspection and Cooling

Grooming and the walk to the grooming station should be a time for a health inspection. You should watch for lameness on the way and check for lumps and bumps while grooming the horse. Swelling and heat should be noticed at this time. The greatest indicator of illness is a change in behavior.

Proper cooling should be practiced. My father's quote about "walking to the barn" is a wise one. It offers the driving horse time to cool down. Cooling the horse's body after a strenuous workout is more important than the recovery of heart rate and respiration.

Here are some tips:

- Walk for the last few minutes.
- Let the horse drink. I have the hostlers offer water in a pail, so the horses get accustomed to taking water from a pail when we are out driving for the day.
- After the harness is removed, hose or sponge the horse with cool water starting with the wheelers that do the most work. Start hosing or sponging the inside of the legs and sides of the neck where the larger blood vessels lie. Scrape off excess water and put the horse in a shaded area.
- You can stand the horse slightly uphill to move the gut organs away from the heart and lungs.
- Observe the horse closely if the horse starts to sweat again repeat the above procedure.
- Fans are helpful in this cooling process.
- Rectal temperature should be no higher than 101 degrees before the horse is put away in the stall, paddock or pasture.
- Hay or grass can be fed immediately after cooling.

Feeding and Disposition

"That horse is feeling its oats," is a common idiom that can apply to any grain-based feed. Oats, corn, barley, and bran–and pelleted and sweet feeds made of that stuff–are all simple carbohydrates (sugars and starches) that pack a high-calorie punch. In horses, simple carbohydrates are broken down in the stomach and absorbed through the small intestines in a matter of hours. Within 40 minutes, at most, to move through the stomach, these carbs can start getting into the bloodstream and affecting a horse very quickly. Essentially, that exuberant equine behavior in the hours after a feed is a sugar-high.

It may be worse with certain types of grains than others. For example, corn (and barley, too) does not have a fibrous hull like oats do, making it a higher-calorie, more concentrated energy source. So, if you substitute corn for oats and feed it in the same amount, you are giving your horse more calories in the same scoop of feed. It's the higher caloric content in certain types of feed that gives your horse an even greater energy boost.

Besides the fact that grain-based feeds are dense in calories, they are also hard on the equine's digestive system. When overfed (a single meal of more than 4-5 pounds at once), undigested starch moves too quickly through the intestines to be properly digested and poses a risk to hindgut health. For both those reasons, one of the best ways to manage your horse's energy level–and overall health–is to increase forage and decrease concentrated feeds. Tryptophan is sometimes introduced into horse feed to quiet an overenergized horse.

Feeding and Level of Work

Quality grass hays, and pasture grass, of course, are a great way to get horses the nutrition they need–and they are digested slowly over a matter of days in the hindgut. This provides a steady source of energy, without the sugar highs, and it is a lot healthier for your horse too.

The majority of our horses are fed some grain-based feed, which we think they need for nutritional reasons and to meet their caloric needs. In addition to the sugar-high and unruly behavior that can happen immediately after feeding, horses can simply be a bundle of too much energy around the clock. While some horses are naturally more high-strung, more often than not, this is evidence of one or both of these causes:

- The horse is consuming more calories than it needs for its activity level.
- The horse is in great physical condition.

If your horse always has energy to burn, the issue may simply be that it is getting more energy than it needs from its feed for the level of work it does. Understanding and managing this balance is key to getting the performance you want.

Keep in mind that a fit horse is naturally a more energetic horse. Thoroughbred racehorses are a great example of this concept. They are overly energetic because they are in top condition–not because they are fed high-protein alfalfa instead of timothy hay.

If your horse truly does need more calories than what's available in grass or hay due to a high activity level, consider feeding beet pulp instead of more grain. Beet pulp is a high-calorie yet healthy feed because it is forage that is easily digested in the hindgut. Also, feeds higher in fat rather than carbs are less likely to cause that after-meal sugar high.

Horses on restricted diets or not fed a feed with supplements added, need to be offered some supplement to get the minerals needed for good health and proper energy. Check with your veterinarian for requirements in your geographic region.

A Happy Horse

To produce a happy horse that understands its handler, the hostlers and driver have to be consistent in the application of the communication aids. A good relationship requires daily human interaction and daily routine work. The equine's behavior is also influenced by the personality and emotional state of the handler. If the handlers are happy, confident, and relaxed individuals, horses benefit.

Bonding and good communication depend on time, consistency, and repetition and the calm, even demeanor of handlers. The brain chemistry of both the horse and human are altered through proximity and touching. This is just another reason why the grooming and ground care of the horse is important.

Happy horses have to have buddies–horse friends and human friends. They also need roughage (grass and hay), fresh water, and visual stimulation which is best met by being outside. Fresh air is a component of happiness. Boredom and uninteresting surroundings are a threat to happiness.

The driving horse has to be comfortable with well-fitted harness, bridle and bit.

Exercise is proven to produce happiness in people and also in horses. That movement not only keeps their body, but each step helps their feet get good blood supply. The movement also helps the digestion process.

Horses also need some downtime. Often after several demanding days drive, like at Newport, Rhode Island, we give the horses time off. On a normal basis, we drive five days a week, so the weekend is an important time off. If there is a weekend show, the horses get time off during the week.

Remember to keep the horse happy and also remember that the training of happy horses requires repetition, repetition, repetition….. and horses like repetition.

TRANSLATING RIDING TO DRIVING

French Riding Master

François Robichon de La Guérinière expressed it this way: "The knowledge of the nature of the horse is one of the first foundations of the art of riding (or driving - my addition) it and every horseman must make it his principle study." La Guérinière knew the foundation to good communication with the horse as stated in his work, L'École de Cavalerie "The School of Horsemanship" on dressage in 1729 and 1731.

De La Gueriniere was a riding master and one of the most influential writers on the art of dressage. Dressage was originally used to train war horses. This precise type of riding evolved into an art form used for training horses and performances were held for the wealthy aristocrats of Europe. His book became an important text for the popular Spanish Riding School in Vienna, Austria.

I believe it is important for the carriage driver to have a basic working knowledge of ridden dressage to understand balance, lightness, obedience, impulsion, and calmness needed to keep the horse happy and pleasurable to the driver. It is helpful to understand the reinsmanship, seat, and legs of the rider and then transfer this knowledge into the aids used by the driver–reins, voice, and whip.

GroundWork

Many of the principles for working saddle horses are true for driving horses. In driving, one needs to include voice commands in training. When leading a driving horse, I advise using the same verbal cues that are used when on the box seat (driver's seat).

Ground driving *can* take place before mounting a saddle horse, but it is *imperative* in teaching the horse to drive. Consequently, the use of the voice is very important during this process.

Here are some steps in the groundwork involved in training the driving horse:

- Fitting the harness and getting the horse accustom to the feel of the harness.
- Ground drive with the harness.
- Move forward.
- Turning.
- Stopping and standing.
- Simulating the cart.
- Simulating pulling and holding back.
- Roadside work.
- Simulating the carriage.

I am not going to talk about training the horse to drive in this book. Many videos on the internet give instruction on basic harnessing and training the horse to drive. My focus will be on helping the driver to better understand and communicate with the driving horse. I will concentrate more on the use of the aids for driving.

The Aids in Riding

The order of the aids is important. The aids are given to the horse in this order:

🐎 **The Legs**: The legs are used primarily as driving aids and ask the horse to move his hind legs under himself. The legs "turn on the engine."

🐎 **The Seat**: The seat guides the horse's body to the hands. The rider's seat directs the energy flow coming from the hind legs and connects the horse's front and hind ends through his back.

🐎 **The Hands**: It is said in riding that "the hands belong to the horse." It is important to ride with soft hands that receive the energy of the horse that comes to the bit. With the communication/feel coming to the hands from the bit, the rider then starts over again with leg aids.

The Aids in Driving

🐎 **The Reins**: There are many methods of holding reins. It is important to learn how to hold the reins and use them correctly for the horse to respond appropriately. A rein board is a great way to practice. As with riding, soft, receiving hands are important.

🐎 **The Voice**: Unlike ridden dressage, where the voice is not allowed, the voice is imperative for driving. The horse needs to learn your various voice commands for the gaits and will learn to rely on your voice for security too.

🐎 **The Whip**: The whip is an extension of the leg and seat. You and your horse need to learn how to communicate with the whip.

What the Horse Experiences

The riding horse can:

- Experience the weight of the rider.
- Feel the rider's legs, seat, and heels.
- See the rider and the rider's hands.
- Carry a lighter bridle.
- Have reins that are shorter and lighter.
- Be reined in by the rider
- Often wear a snaffle bit with direct pull.

The driving horse has:

- a feel of the reins.
- Longer reins.
- A heavier bridle.
- The voice of the driver.
- The touch of the whip.
- Often a curb bit.
- The feel of the shafts or pole and other horse (s) in multiple turnouts.
- The sound of the carriage.

Why are Driving Aids Different?

Why are the aids for driving so much different?

- The horse cannot see the person giving commands.
- The horse cannot feel the person giving the commands except through the reins.
- Consequently, the driver's voice and whip replace the legs and seat of the rider.

Is Pressure Different in Driving?

Riders often want the horse to move away from pressure as you see with the western rider applying left leg pressure to get the horse to hold its body up and move to the right.

Interestingly, the carriage driver wants a horse to move into the pressure of the collar and away from pressure or tap of the whip. Also, the driving horse must take the pressure off the breaching and resist moving away from it.

Some Driving is Riding

Demi-Deaumont is a type of turnout where a postilion rider is mounted on the near horse (or left horse) of a pair of horses. Grand Deaumont is the expansion of four horses where postilion riders direct four horses from atop the near horse of each pair.

The mounted horse is called the ride horse, and the companion horse in each pair is called the hand horse. This off horse (or right-hand horse) has only a forked connector to only one rein that runs to the rider's hand. Essentially, the rider carries three reins in his or her left hand and carries a postilion (short) whip in the right hand. This whip is used to tap the hand horse on the shoulder or hip to encourage movement to or away from the rider, and to encourage the hand horse to move forward since it lacks the pressure of the rider's legs to direct it.

Both the ride horse and the hand horse wear typical driving bridles and bits. The saddle pads are bedecked with a crest of the household that is presenting the turnout. The ranking postilion rider is mounted on the wheel horse (the one closest to the wheels of the carriage).

The most significant people ride facing forward inside the carriage. Those of lesser status will ride facing backward in this French-made caleche.

Often, a footman will ride in a rear seat or stand on a platform if traveling a short distance. Two mounted outriders will precede this turnout to clear the way. Other horse hostlers will walk beside each horse or a pair of horses to assist with keeping the horses calm or still at the halt and make sure the bridles remain in place.

Posture

Riding Posture

- As you ride, your legs should hang down from your hips — in a position that would allow you to stand "on your own two feet" if your horse wasn't there to hold you.
- Legs are relaxed and hanging just behind the horse's girth.
- You can draw a straight line through the rider's ear, shoulder, hip, and heel.

Driving Posture

- The upper body and spine must be straight. The development of core muscles is extremely important to sit on the box seat for hours at a time such as is the custom with carriage drivers. The driver's seat typically does not have a back so that the driver can lean back when needed. This is requiring more when driving pairs and multiples than when driving a single horse.
- The arms should rest comfortably at the driver's side so when the upper body is rotated the arms go with the body.
- A good driver uses his or her entire body when driving–eyes, head, shoulders, legs, and feet.
- The lower body often works in the opposite direction of the upper body to brace against the toe board.
- The driver's eyes are in the direction of the turn. Where the eyes go, the head goes where the head goes the horses go. The driver's eyes should never look down. The horse should follow its head, and the driver should follow his eyes.
- The reins have to be gripped, but the fingers have to remain flexible to give signals.

Engagement of the Horse

Engagement of the horse is important in driving just as in riding. Engagement is a process whereby the horse, through the use of its core muscles, can work from its back end to its front for impulsion and forward movement. This is needed to make sure the horse stays balanced over its feet for a forward movement, particularly at the trot where the diagonal feet strike the ground at the same time.

We might consider it being like a car with rear-wheel drive. It is the pushing from the rear quarters and belly muscles which elevates its back and rounding down through its neck which moves it forward onto the bit.

Where did we hear of core muscles before? We heard it when I talked about the posture of the person who is dancing or in the driver's seat of the carriage. To biomechanically move one's body properly, these muscles have to be used effectively.

The trick in driving is to get the horse to move into the bit properly without pulling on the driver's hand. Some conformational characteristics make this easier for some horses to engage. Baroque horses have less difficulty in achieving this balance since they have been bred for generations to execute a proper trot. Ponies with long necks are also well-suited for driving.

If you crossbreed horses for driving, it is important that you cross two trotting breeds such as the Morgan-Friesian or Saddlebred-Andalusian.

Understand the Gaits

The WALK is a four-beat diagonal gait that has been perfected in workhorses that have to pull heavy loads. However, all horses can do this gait. Draft horse breeds like Percherons, Belgium, and Clydesdales are particularly good at this gait.

The TROT is a two-beat diagonal gait that is the primary gait of the carriage horse since it is the most sustainable gait over distance. Warmbloods, Morgans, Saddlebreds, Friesians, Spanish, Lusitanos and most pony breeds are exceptionally good with this gait.

The CANTER is essentially a three-beat gait that has been perfected in herding horses for sprint work and race horses for distances of a furlong to a mile and one half. The Arabians, Quarter Horses, and Thoroughbreds are fast and talented with this gait.

The AMBLE is a four-beat lateral gait that is comfortable for riding distances on the back of a horse in a saddle. Paso Finos, Tennessee Walkers, Missouri Foxtrotters, Rocky Mountain Horses and Icelandic Ponies are gifted with this gait that is so smooth for the rider who might be in the saddle.

The REINBACK, which if properly executed, is two beat diagonal steps backward.

The HALT is when the horse stops balanced over all four feet. When not in show circumstances, drivers like to see the horse rest one hind foot by moving its weight to a supporting leg.

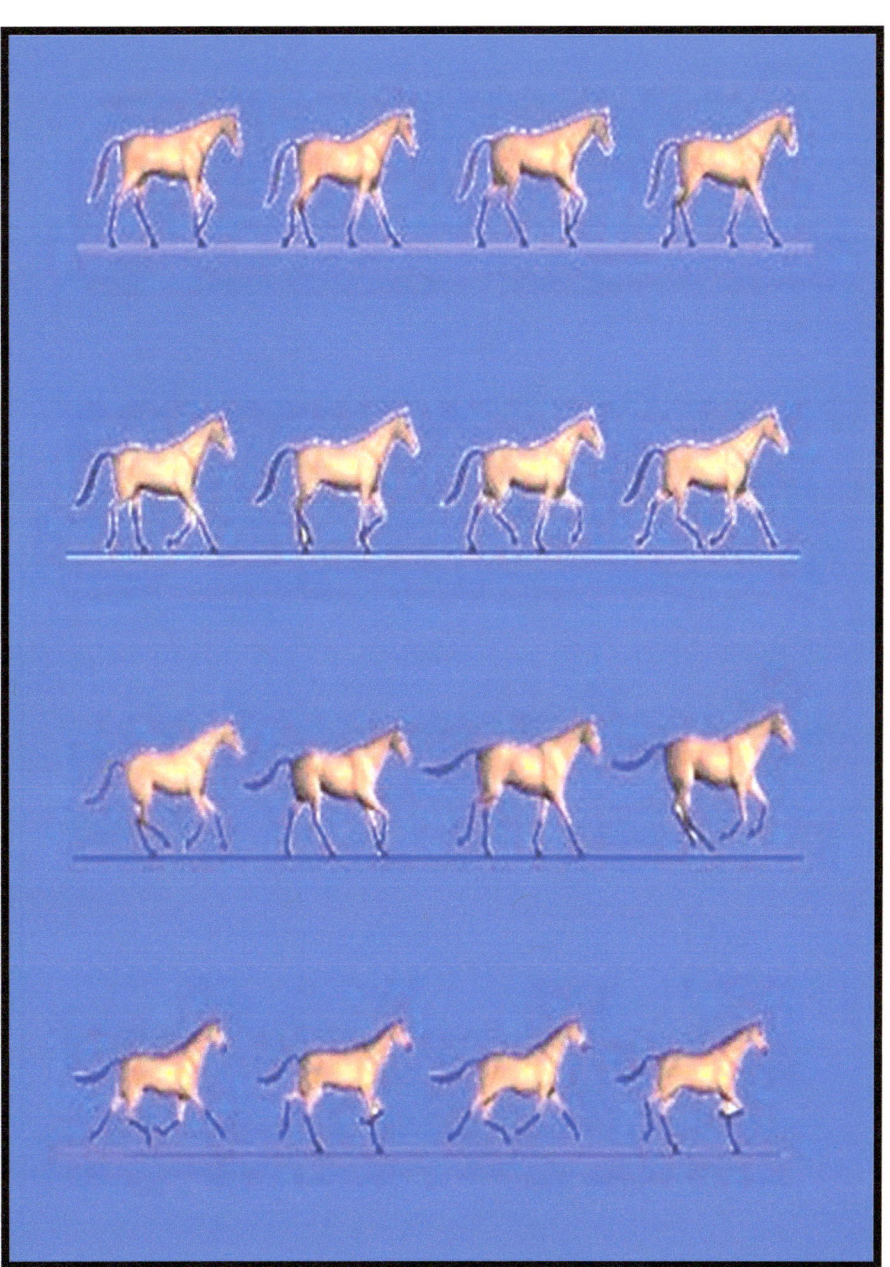

The Importance of the Trot

The gait of the carriage horse throughout history has been the trot. It is the most sustainable gait over distance. I routinely exercise my horses driving 6 to 8 miles at a trot without stopping. Polo ponies that canter throughout a chukker are exercised at the trot to build endurance. Endurance horses may canter at times but, perform most of the route at a trot.

Our towns are mainly 8 miles apart which is a comfortable trotting distance for a horse in one hour without stopping. The horse could be rested and perhaps watered before traveling on or returning to its home stable.

Today, in driven dressage, we refer to the working, collected and extended trot or in pleasure driving we call it working, slow or strong trot. All in all, it is what was practiced years ago when the working trot would be used to go to town, the slow trot with a salute might be used when meeting someone on the roadway, and the strong trot might be used when late on the return trip home.

Speed limits might be established by the trot because it was an easy way to tell if the horse and carriage were traveling at about 8 miles per hour. Pleasure driving requires that the horse stays at the trot to assure it is not approaching a dangerous speed with a carriage. Years ago, horses might be sprung (cantered) up the hill to get extra momentum with a load, but the normal gait was the trot.

Bending and Balance

Riding horses must bend and driving horses must bend too! Just because they are between shafts does not mean that they should not and cannot bend.

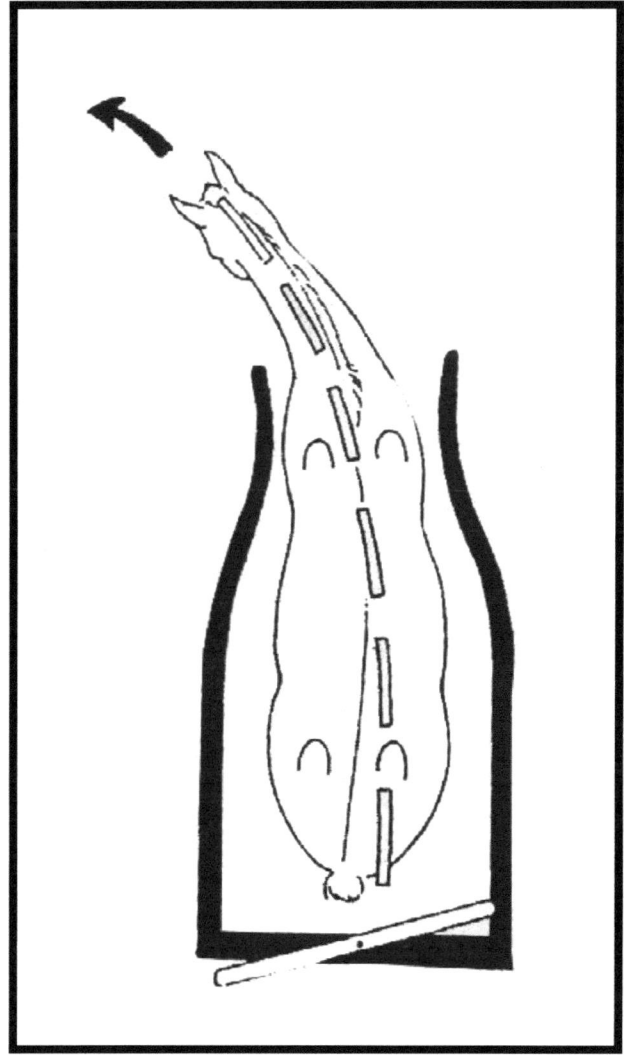

The driving horse must:

- Perform without the aid of a rider.
- Follow his head.
- Sometimes move forward without following its head.
- Become relaxed and at other times become engaged.
- Be capable of elongating and shortening its frame.
- Bend in the direction of the turn and sometimes, upon command, counter bend into the turn.
- Move into pressure and resist pressure.
- Stay balanced over their feet.
- Move laterally in either direction.

It is our job as the "whip" (driver) to help the driving horse do all of these things. As in riding, driving is a partnership between horse and human!

Yielding to the Bit

A horse can only yield to the bit if the horse is truly engaged.

Previously I spoke about engagement. Engagement of the horse is important in driving just as in riding. Engagement is a process whereby the horse, through the use of its core muscles, can work from its back end to its front for impulsion and forward movement. An engaged horse will be light and responsive to the bit because when the horse engages onto the ring of muscles as described above, the neck arches and the jaw relaxes, giving the feeling that the horse is softening onto the bit as opposed to resisting against it.

No amount of "fiddling" with the reins will produce engagement. So before we talk about yielding to the bit we need to make sure that our horse is engaged; only then can we expect the horse to respond to the rein aids properly.

Inside and Outside Rein

When riding, acceptance of the contact is the horse's responsibility, and it's the rider's job to tell him it's his job. Horses are not like cars that stay in gear; horses need reminding by using effective aids. In driving it is equally important for the horse to accept the contact and respond.

Use of the reins when driving:

- Pull or squeeze on a rein until the horse moves its head (yields) in the direction of the pull.
- Sometimes this requires a steady pull or sometimes "nagging" until the horse's head stays in the desired position and the horse's body is in the frame and following through (engaged).
- Stop the pressure, or the nagging, when the horse yields with its head and body in the correct frame (engaged).

Inside rein the first one activated controls:

- Bend of the neck.
- Elevation of the horses head.

Outside rein used in conjunction with inside rein effects:

- Flexion at the pole.
- Speed (extension) of the feet.
- Either or both reins affect the placement of the feet.

Half-halt

In riding a half-halt is defined as follows: "The half-halt is the hardly visible, almost simultaneous, coordinated action of the seat, the legs and the hand of the rider, with the object of increasing the attention and balance of the horse before the execution of several movements or transitions between gaits or paces. In shifting slightly more weight onto the horse's quarters, the engagement of the hind legs and the balance on the haunches are facilitated for the benefit of the lightness of the forehand and the horse's balance as a whole." [USEF Rule Book DR108]

In driving a half-halt is used for the same purpose; to rebalance the horse and prepare him for a change and to get his attention. In driving we do not have the seat and legs, so we activate the rein with slight tweaking, little tugs, flexing your finger, or squeezing the rein. It is often used in conjunction with the whip. In driving, the whip takes the place of the leg and seat

Half-halts for Communication

- Tug or double half-halt inside rein to bend in the direction of the turn.
- Release outside rein to go in the direction of the head.
- Both inside rein and outside rein effect a change of rein.
- Both inside rein and outside rein effect lateral movement.

Coordinate Half-halts with Raised Front Leg

- Take advantage of the elevated leg to tug the horse off balance to one side or the other.
- Bend left, half-halt left rein when the left front leg is raised and horse steps left.
- Bend left, half-halt right rein when the right front leg is raised and horse steps right.

The Sequence of the Left Turn
A Three-step Process

- Half-halt the inside rein to establish a bend (the horse is still moving forward).
- Release outside rein (move the right hand slightly forward) to go in the direction of the turn when ready.
- Half-halts or slight pressure with either rein is used to control the footfalls to the right or left without changing reins. (See Lateral Movements.)

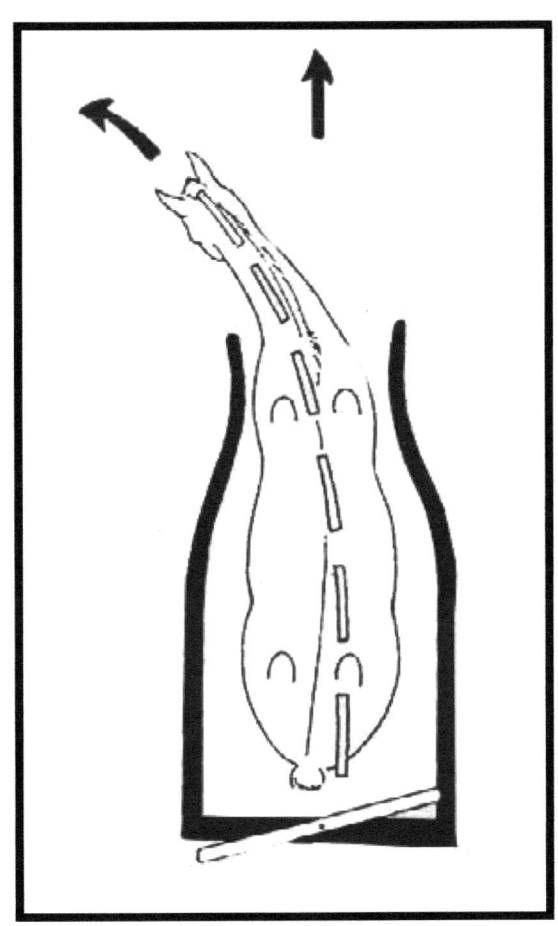  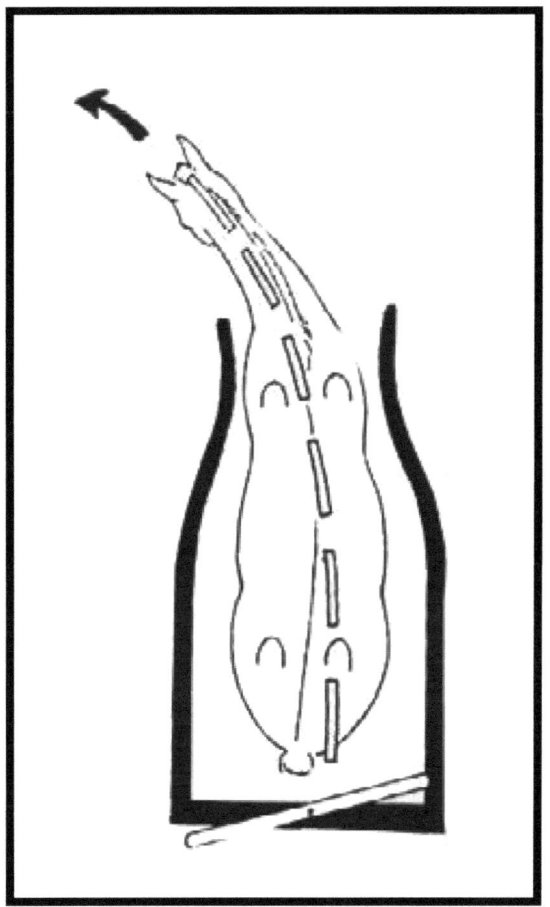

The Sequence of the Right Turn
A Three-step Process

- Half-halt inside rein to establish bend (the horse still moving forward).
- Then release outside rein to go in the direction of the turn.
- Half-halts or slight pressure with either rein is used to control the footfalls to the right or left without changing reins. (See Lateral Movements.)

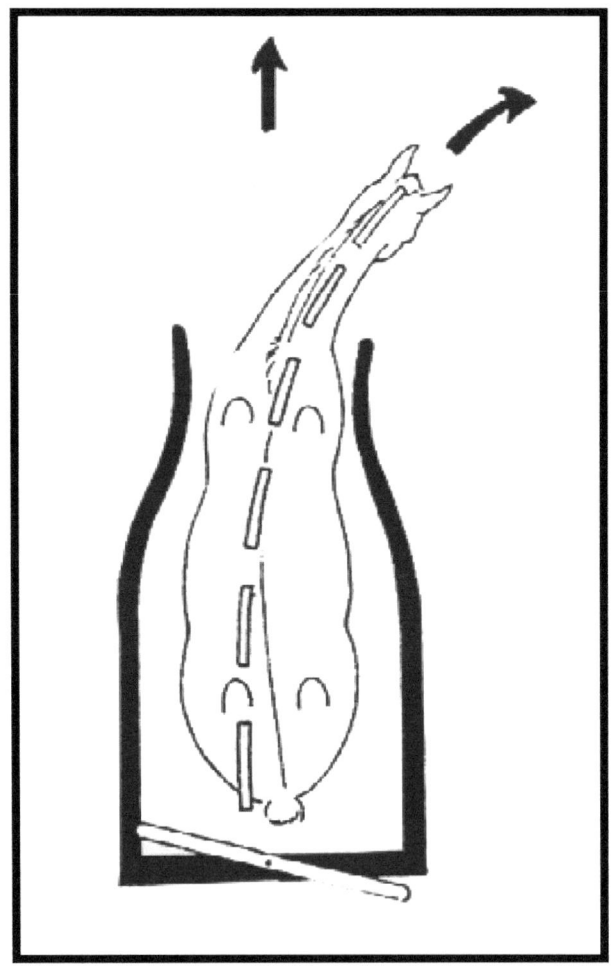

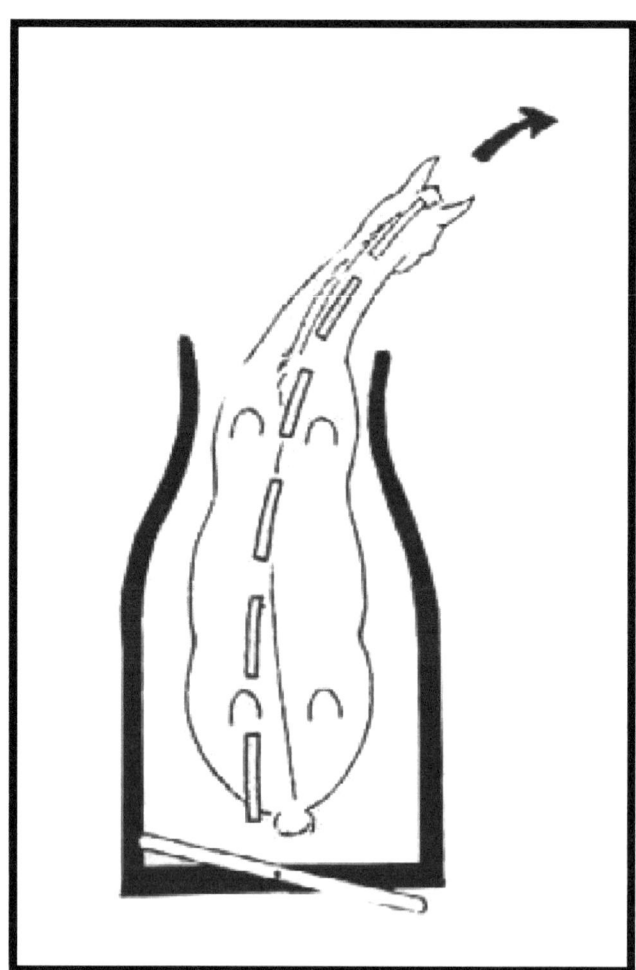

Lateral Movements

In riding, lateral movements consist of gymnastic exercises such as shoulder-in, haunches-in and the derived exercises like renvers, half pass, and pirouette. These exercises ensure the horse to develop symmetrically in body and limbs and prepare the horse for collection.

While the driving horse does not do the gymnastic exercises in harness, it is still important that the horse be able to move laterally. If we need to turn a two-wheeled vehicle in a tight space, the horse needs to be able to move laterally to pivot the vehicle on its axle.

To achieve lateral movement the driving horse must:

- Have impulsion and balance.
- Follow the bit.
- Yield to the bit.
- Bend.
- Respond to a half-halt.

Lateral Movements - Right and Left

The basic lateral movements for the driving horse are moving left and right.

- 🐎 While bent to the left, but moving to the right, hold the inside rein steady and half-halt the right rein when the right front foot is elevated to move the horse to the right.
- 🐎 While bending to the left and moving left, hold the outside rein steady and half-halt the inside rein when the left front foot is elevated to move the horse to the left.

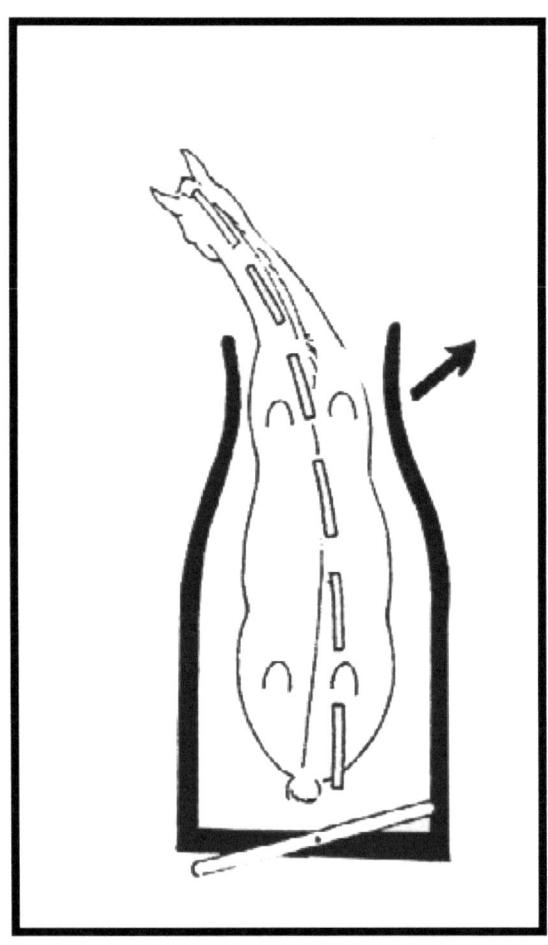

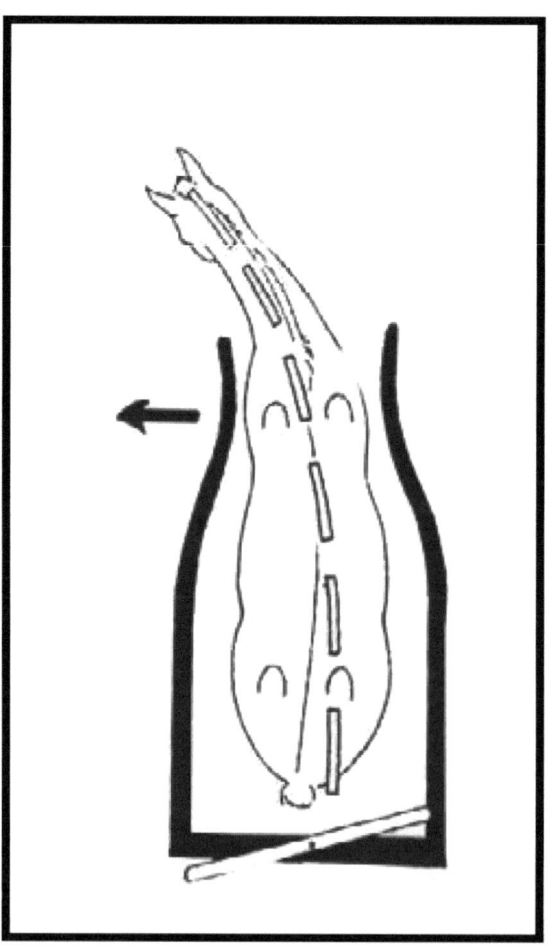

Circles, Corners, and Turns

When riding, our legs, seat, and hands are the aids that we use to communicate to the horse that we want to turn or make a circle. We will talk about the aids used for driving in the next section. A well-trained driving horse and skilled whip can also make turns and circles even without the use of the seat and legs.

When preparing for an upcoming turn, half-halt first in the direction of the turn to signal the horse to "yield to the bit." Turn its head by bending its neck in the direction of the turn and follow his head.

Once the horse is bending in the right direction, work (half-halt) either the inside or outside reins, depending on the guidance needed.

The corners of a show ring or dressage arena are properly sequenced to do these turns. The first step is to ask the horse to bend in the direction of the upcoming turn but go straight by holding or working the outside rein to keep the horse from following his head too soon. The second step is to release the outside rein by moving the hand slightly forward at the point you want the horse to follow his head. The driver is working the reins with slight tugs or slight pressure on the inside or the outside rein to control each footfall. Corners are lateral movements into the corner to prevent the horse from turning too soon.

To straighten the horse, just sit back or bring your reins/arms back to a level position.

Bring the arm up and to the center or across the body, to shorten the inside rein, whereas extending the opposite arm lengthens the outside rein.

The driver is almost constantly sending messages with the body to direct the horse. If the horse is doing exactly the correct thing, do nothing. Just keep your hands, arms, and body still.

A Good Rider or Driver

A good rider or driver:

🐎 Has bonded with the horse and developed trust.

🐎 Can read the horse's body language.

🐎 Can stay relaxed and calm around the horse(s).

🐎 Knows how to desensitize a horse to scary things.

🐎 Knows the aids and how and when to use them.

🐎 Understands balance, impulsion, and footfalls.

🐎 Can establish an even cadence and move to collection and extension keeping the same cadence, lengthens and shortens the stride and makes various maneuvers keeping the same cadence.

🐎 Knows that carriage brakes do not stop the horse. They only save the horse work in slowing and stopping the carriage, and they smooth the transitions from one gait to another.

🐎 Is always initiating movement or lack of movement.

🐎 Can execute lateral movements and understand the placement of the feet.

🐎 Remains calm and never angers.

TALKING WITH TACK

The Aids and the Tack for Driving

- The bit.
- The reins - reins affect the front of the body.
- The voice - voice aids impulsion, direction, and cadence.
- The whip - whip affects the entire body, but mainly the hindquarters.
- The harness.

Why the Bit is Important

Some truths:

- The mouth and lips of the horse are very sensitive.
- 60% of its weight is in front of girth.
- 90% of its balance is in the head and neck.
- If you control the head and neck, you can control the horse.

For the bit to work effectively, the bit should be comfortable and fit properly. The horse should not fear the bit because our goal is to get the horse to go forward into the bit so that the slightest of tugs give instructions to the horse.

Since 60-70% of the horse's weight is in front of the girth and 90% of its balance is in its head and neck, a double half halt is used to change reins. A single half halt moves the horses laterally in varying increments while they are still bent in the direction of the turn. Signaling of half halts should correspond with the elevation of the front leg when the horse is at the trot. Since 90% of the balance is in the head and neck, half halting when the right front foot is in the air can move the horse to the right; half halting when the left front leg is in the air can move the horse to the left. This can be done with the horse bent in either direction to achieve lateral movements to the inside or outside of the turn.

Using this system of half halts with a relaxed horse can allow the driver to control each footfall and expand and contract the circle by allowing the horse to move laterally to the right or left in the turn.

Bits are important for

- Communication.
- Attention and control. If you can control the head, you can control the horse.
- Establishing a bend of the neck, elevation of the head, and flexion at the pole.
- Placement of the horse's feet.
- Activating the balance of the horse.
- Engagement and collection are created through the horse's forward movement into the bit without leaning on the bit. The release of pressure is the reward for the horse.

Weight and Balance

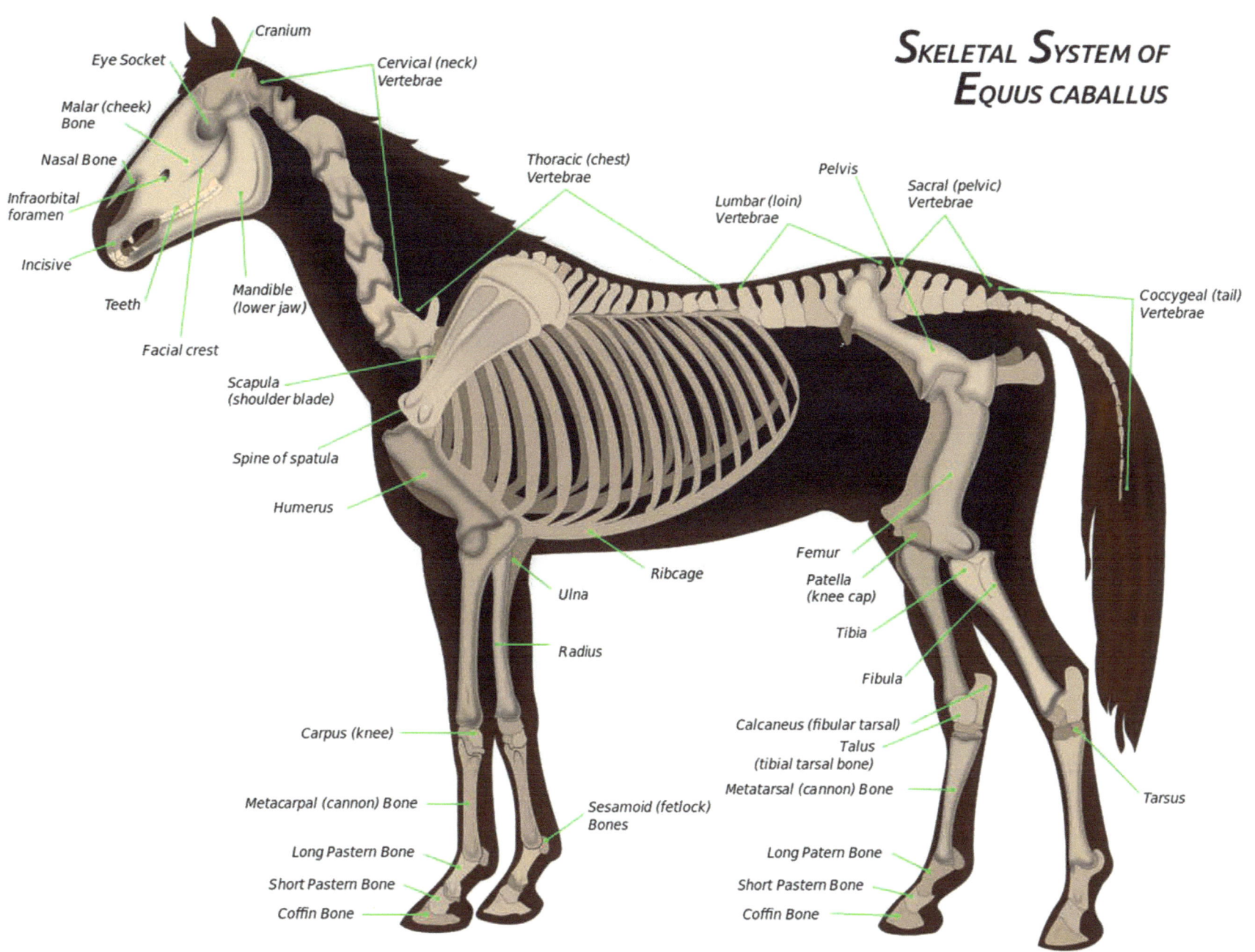

Mechanical Advantage of the Bit

Pictured below is a curb bit, a commonly used driving bit.

Think of the bit as a lever, the position of the reins on the cheek, relative to the mouthpiece and rein attachment location, gives the driver greater mechanical advantage. The diagram below shows the lever as it relates to the bit.

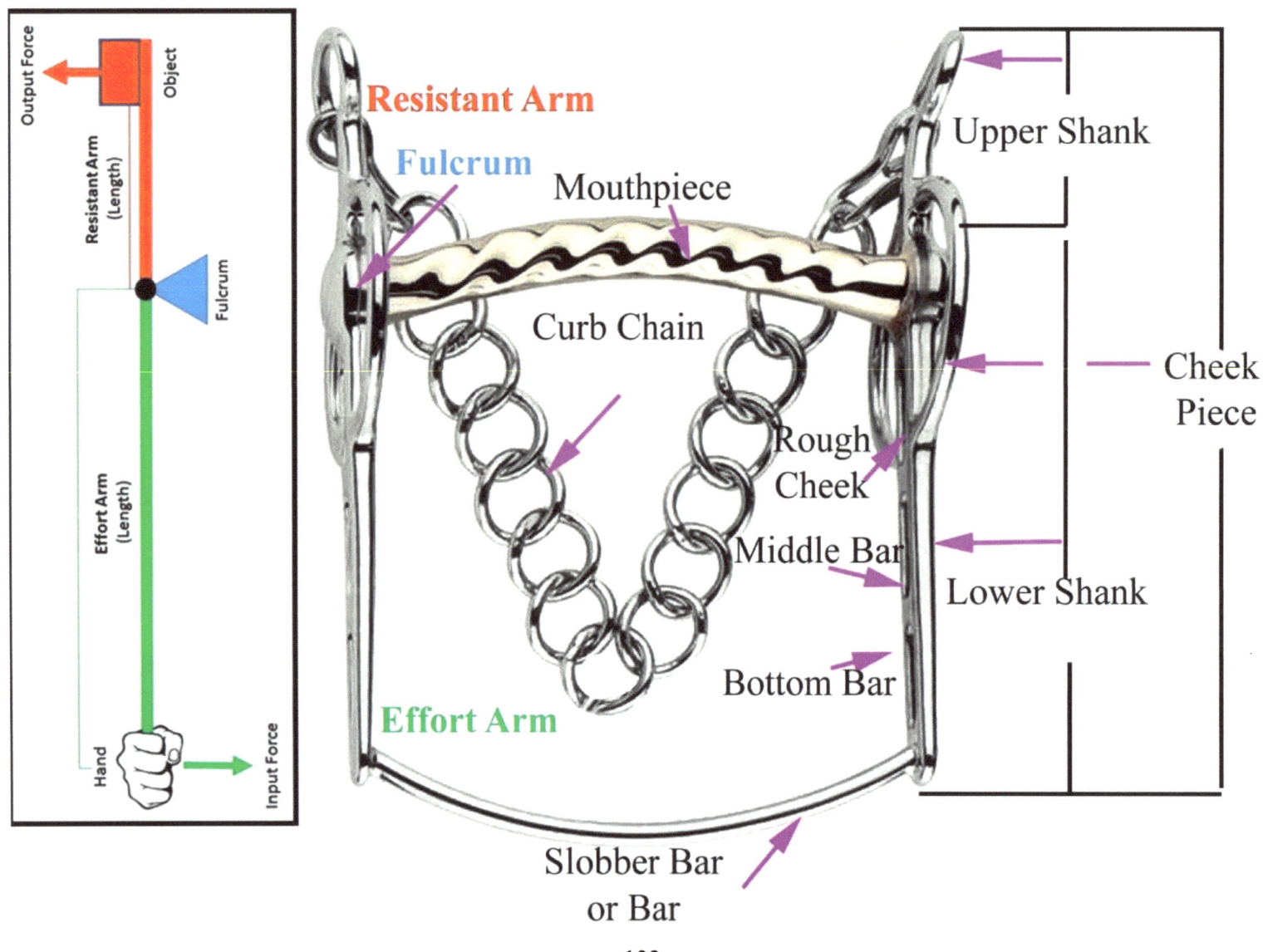

Bit Pressure Points

Curb bits often have a solid mouthpiece and have varying heights of center port. The port either gives relief to the tongue or is used to pressure the palate or both, depending on how high it is. They also apply pressure to the bars of the mouth, the chin, and the poll. *(Diagram courtesy of Horse-Pros.com)*

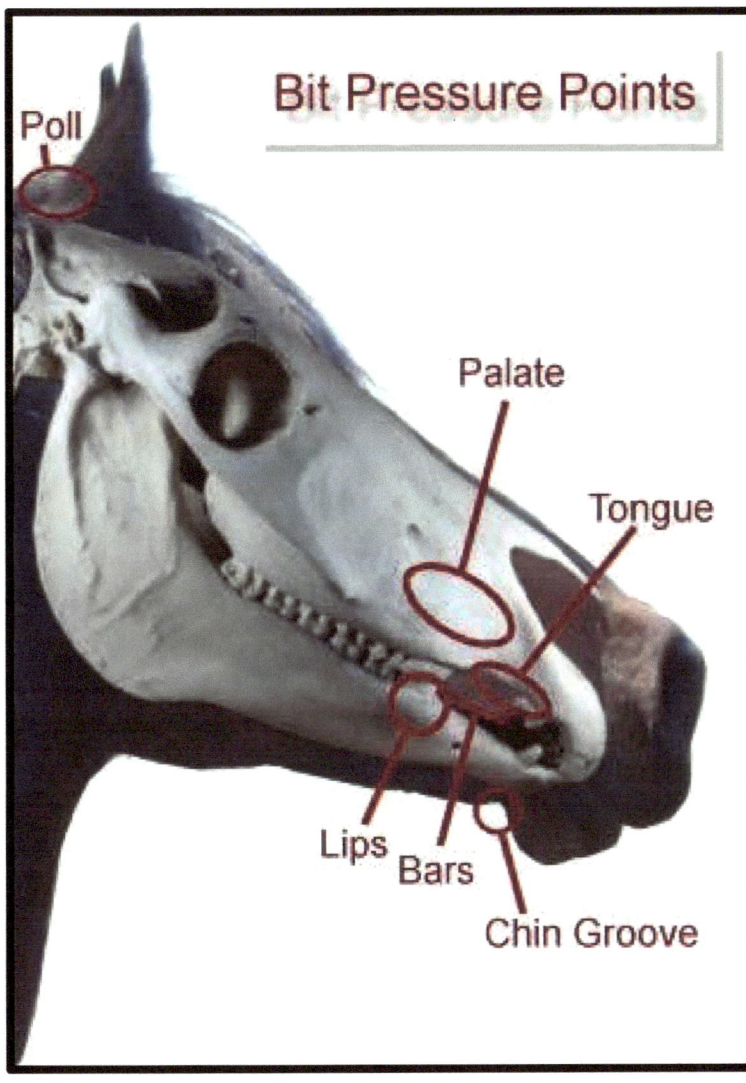
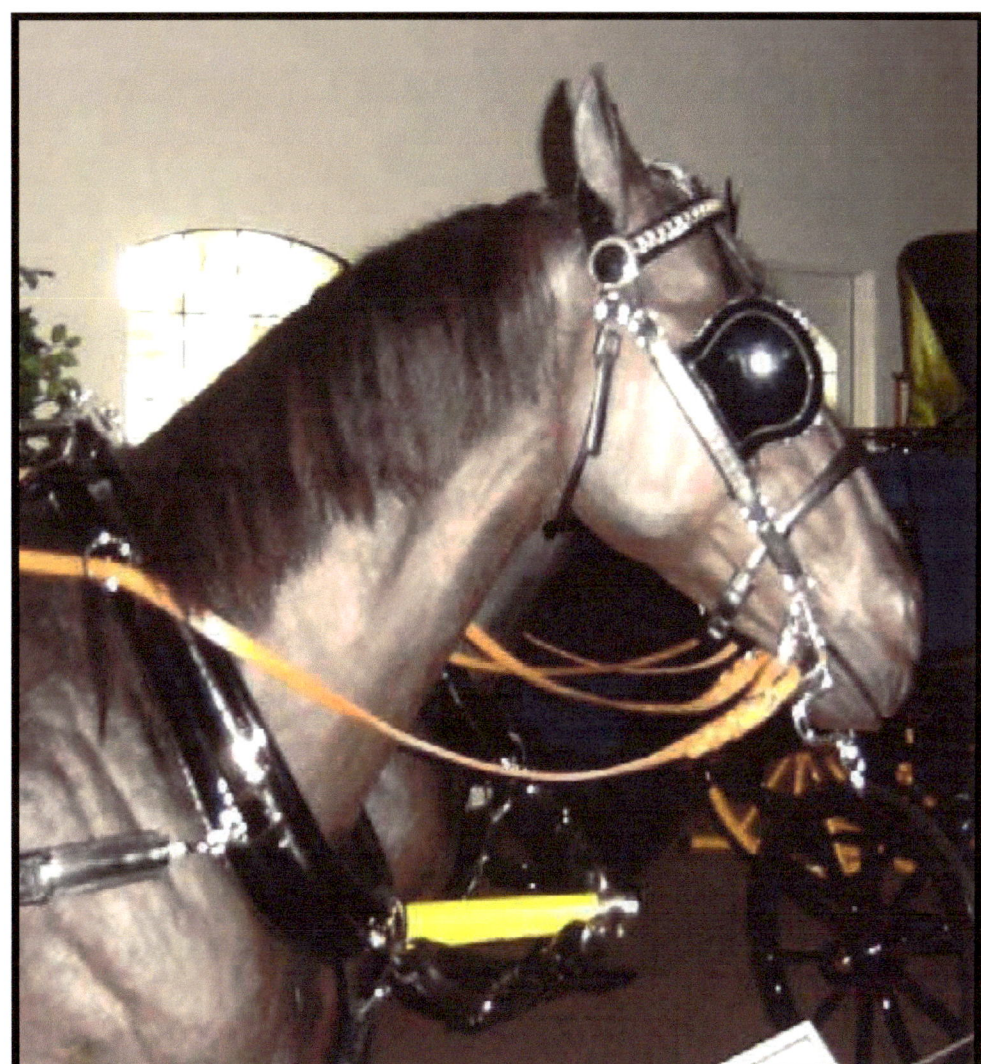

The Driving Bit

Few people understand the definition of a driving bit. A driving bit has to have more than one position for the rein, and there is always a snaffle position. Most driving bits are curb bits because, unless used properly, horses often resist the use of a snaffle and do not come into the frame needed for proper communication. Also, when driving pairs or multiples, the mechanical advantage of a curb is needed.

There are many reasons for multiple positions for the reins. The disposition of a horse in particular situations or environment might warrant the movement of a rein. Also, the training level of the horse or technical proficiency of the driver may necessitate a change of position of the rein on the bit.

The most popular of the driving bits are the Liverpool bits as seen here (bottom right). The large flat circles on the side of the bit make it particularly comfortable when the rein on the opposite side of the horse's face is pulled. The opposing side covers a broad surface around the lips to bring the horses head to the side.

To the left below are four Friesians, and to the right, is a picture of a Kladruby horse from the Czech Republic.

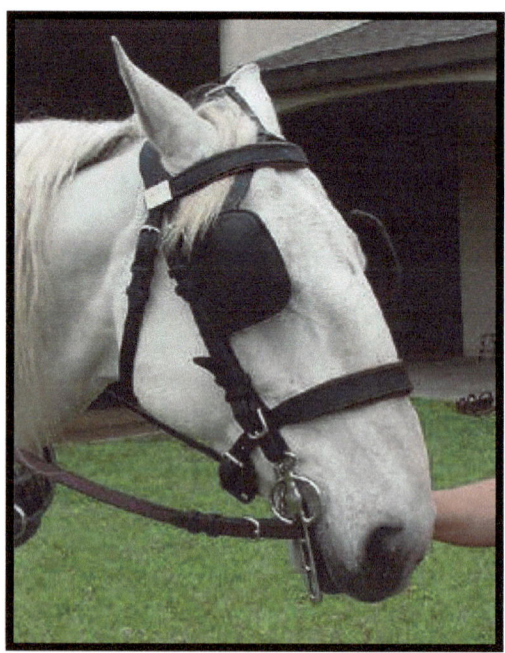

Liverpool Bit

The most common driving bit is a Liverpool cheek piece.

When driving multiples, I prefer a Liverpool with a German Arched mouthpiece and fixed cheek pieces; this just means the cheek piece is fixed on the mouthpiece and does not rotate or move up and down.

I am partial to the German arch because it allows room for the horse's tongue and does not pinch it when the bit is activated. When rotated, the arch rotates forward and leaves room for the horse's tongue, inviting the horse to move forward.

The cavesson, or noseband, should be suspended on separate hangers, just two fingers below the horse's pronounced jaw bone. Why on separate hangers? The cavesson should stay stationary as the cheek pieces rotate forward to apply pole pressure. If the cheek pieces and cavesson are fixed together, the rotation of the upper shank of the curb bit can rub into the jaw of the horse and cause irritation on the inside and outside of the mouth.

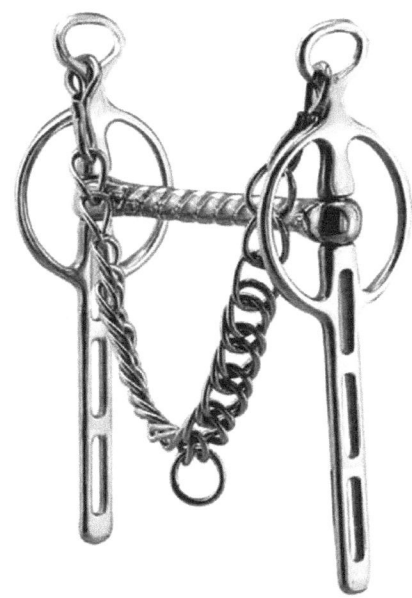

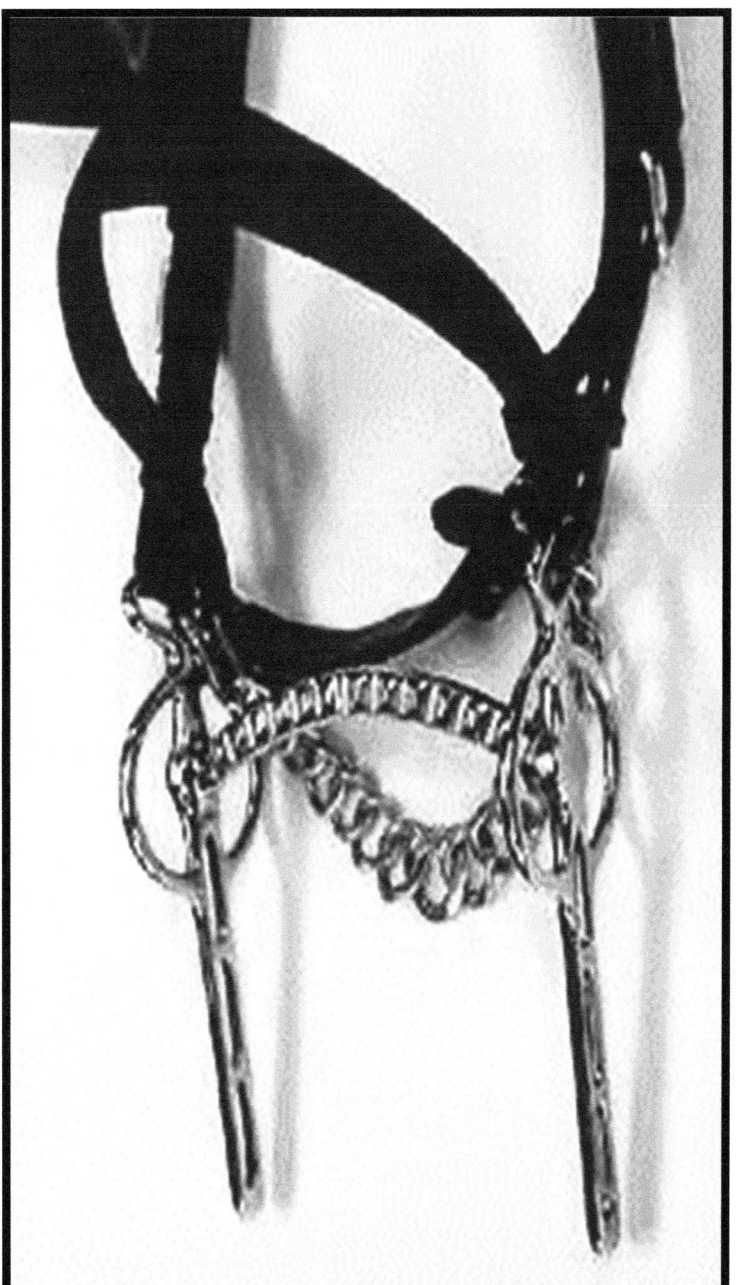

More Driving Bits

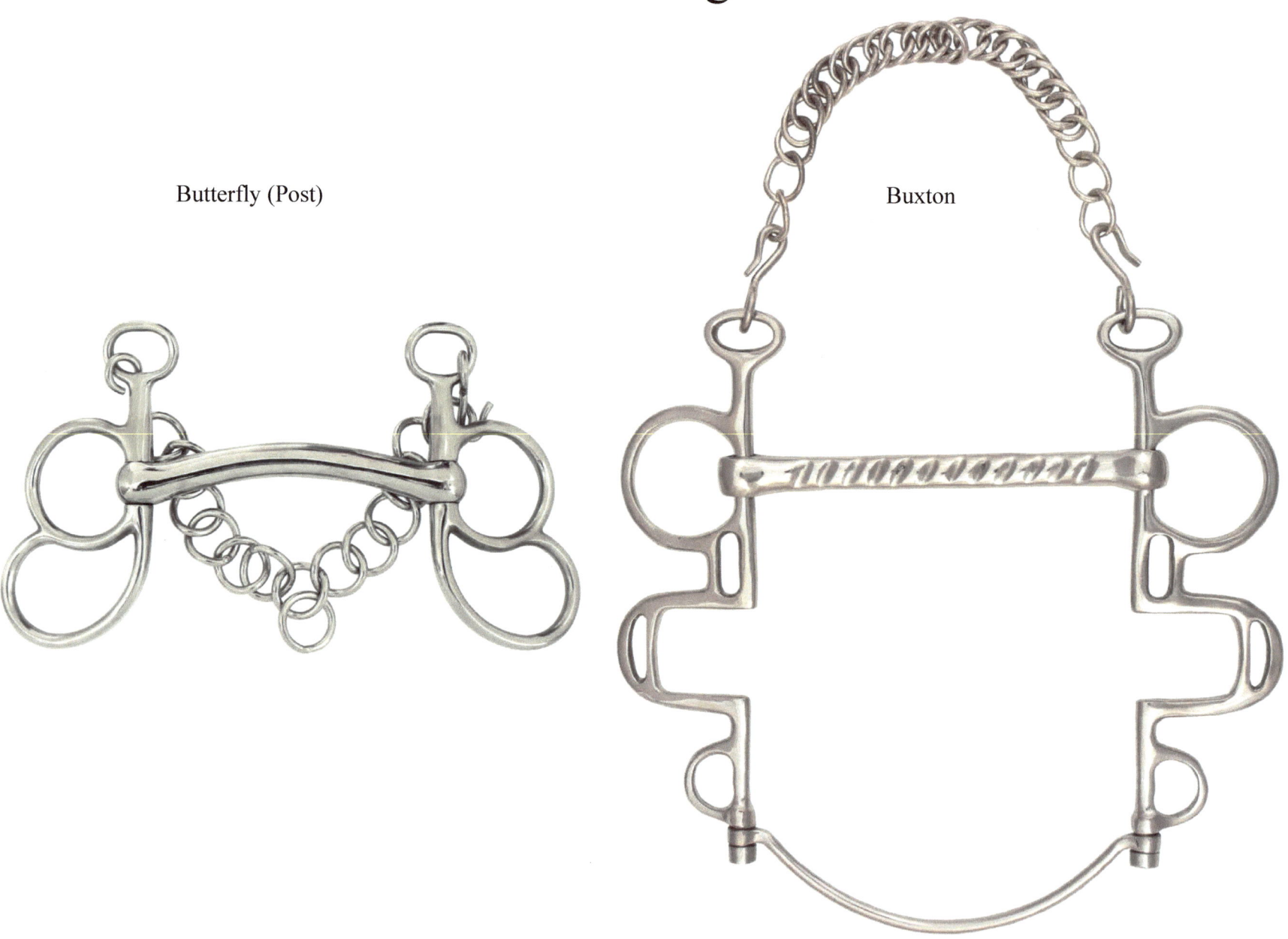

Butterfly (Post)

Buxton

Ashleigh Bit   Wilson Bit

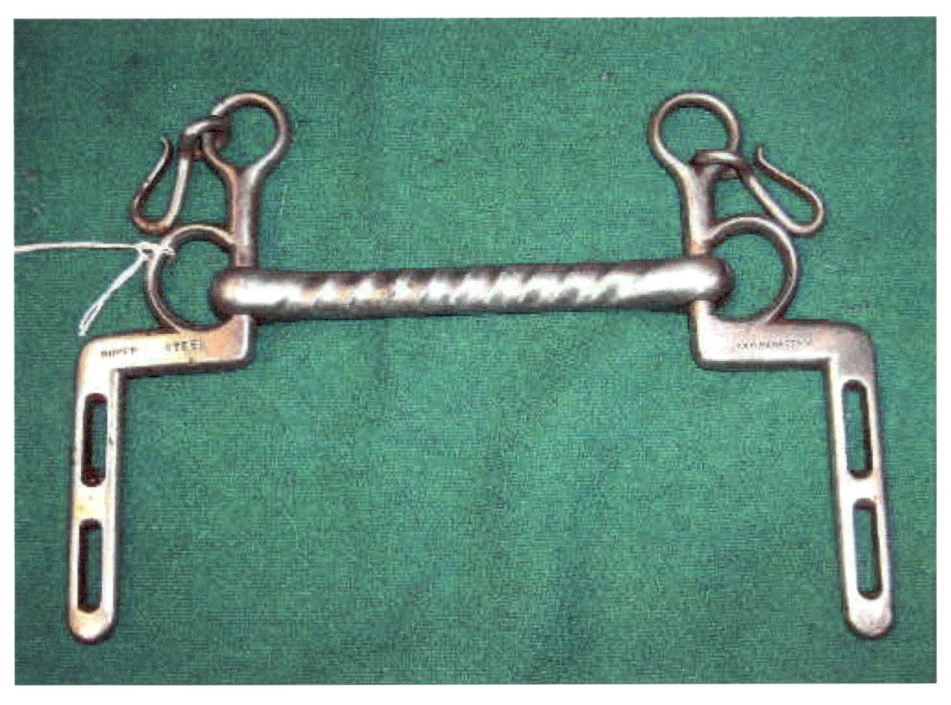

Mouthpieces Come in Many Styles

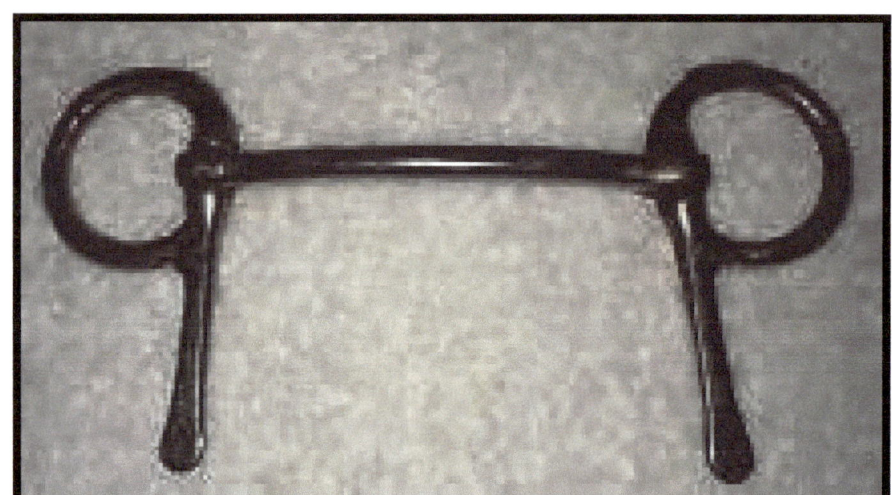

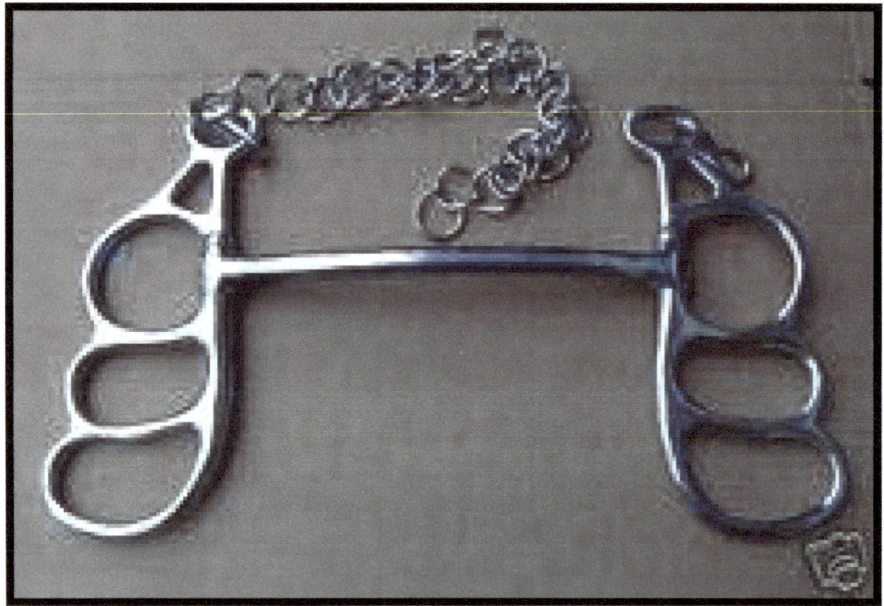

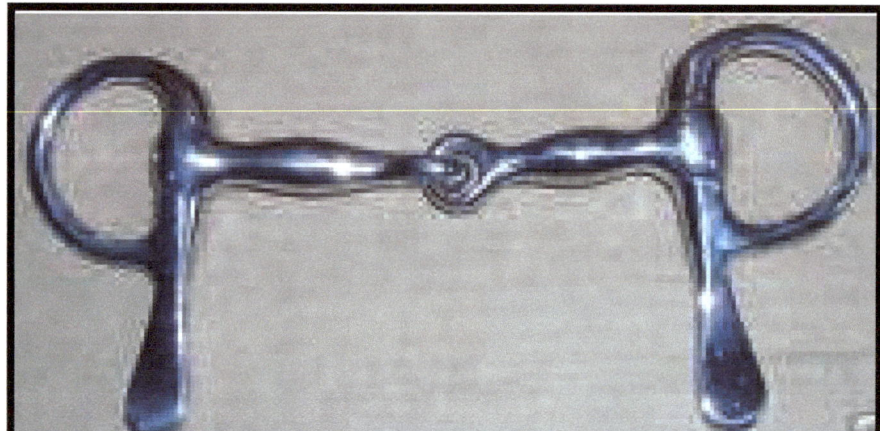

What Is a Bar Bit?

The bit on the right is a Buxton, which is known as a bar bit because it has a metal bar joining the bottoms of each shank. This is to prevent the long shanks of a driving bit from getting caught on the reins and bridle of the adjacent horse. As a precaution of a bar bit getting caught on a shaft, or pole end, or leader bars, the bit on the left has a breakaway plastic tubing affixed to the lower shank.

There are hazards involved with each type. The driver must be aware and choose the type used according to the event.

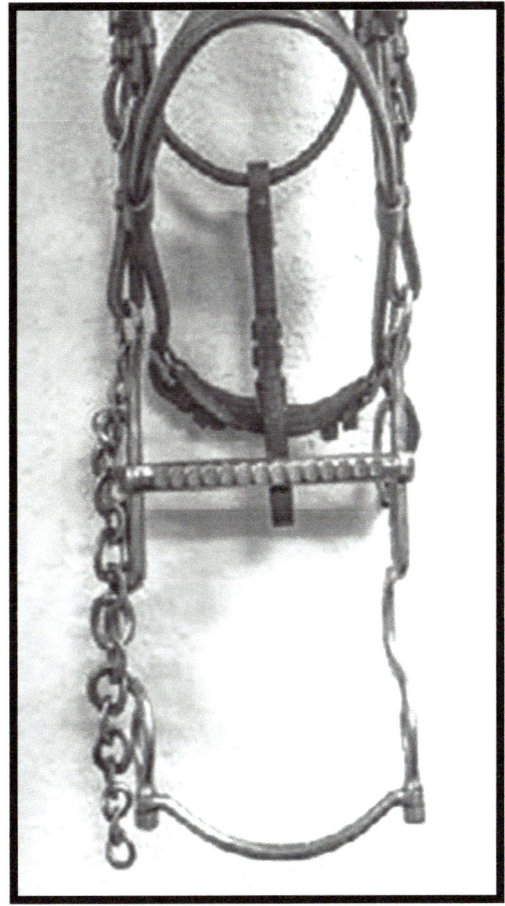

Action of a Snaffle and Driving with Two Bits

- There is only a direct pull from activating a snaffle.
- There is no lever or mechanical advantage with a snaffle.
- The jointed mouthpiece creates a "nutcracker effect" on the horse's jaw.

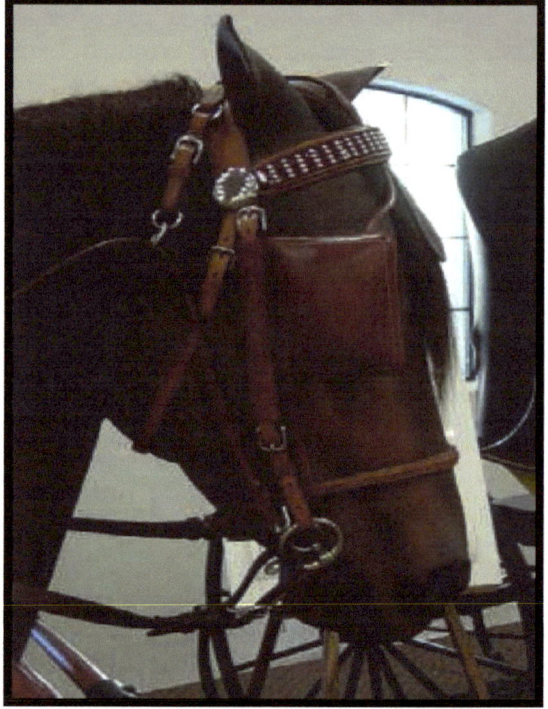

Here's a half-cheek snaffle with a bearing rein and a bradoon bit.

- The mouthpiece can be jointed or straight or slightly curved - e.g., Mullen mouth.
- If the driving bit's mouthpiece is jointed, the bradoon should be straight.
- If the driving bit is straight, the bradoon should be jointed.

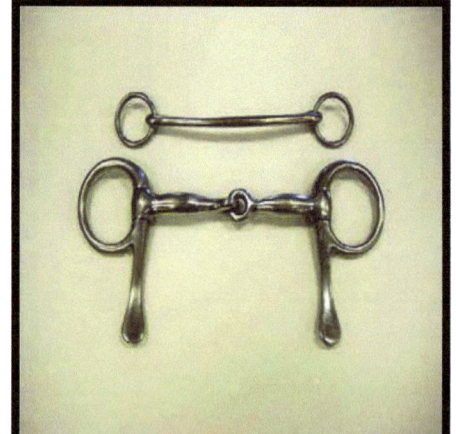

half-cheek snaffle

Rein Position

On a Liverpool bit, there are multiple rein settings (picture to the right). The top position is called Plain Cheek. The second position from the top is called Rough Cheek, which is the most common position for the rein. The third position from the top is called the Middle Bar, and the last position is called the Bottom Bar.

On the post bit, or sometimes called the butterfly bit (picture in the lower right), is a proper driving curb chain with rings that are graduated in diameter from smallest on the sides to largest in the center. This chain can be untwisted to lay flat against the jaw. These flattened links make a smooth, comfortable fit in the chin groove. The curb chain is activated as the lower shank is pulled by the rein toward the driver, and the upper shank rotates forward. The rotation of the upper shank forward applies poll pressure to the top of the horse's head.

When describing a bit, one should label the cheek piece by name, the action of the bit, the style of the mouthpiece, and the presence of a bar at the bottom of the shanks. The bit at the bottom (on the left) is a Buxton cheek curb bit with a straight mouthpiece and a bar.

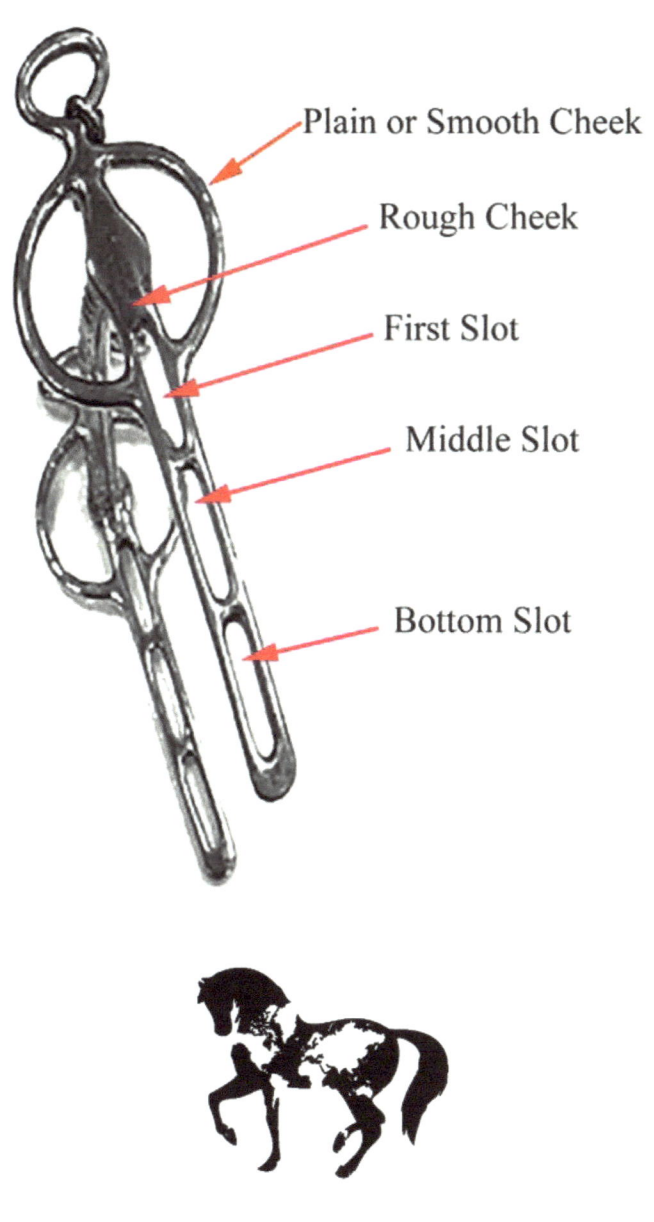

What is Four-in-hand?

It means holding four reins in the left hand and manipulating the reins with the right hand. The right hand controls the inside rein at the beginning of the turns, and the left-hand controls the outside rein. The more dexterous right hand then moves to the inside of outside reins as needed to control the footfalls of the horse. The fingers, wrists, arms, body, and legs are all used. The British coachmen are the originators of the British Hand, and after learning this system, Achenbach recorded it for the German military.

Here you see a picture of my hands doing what is called "covering the reins." The right hand is always held close to the left so the fingers of the right hand can follow the reins forward. Therefore, the driver knows which rein to grasp. It is important that the drivers not look at their hands while driving, so this system of following the reins and picking the one needed is followed. All the fingers of both hands are used when driving a four or what carriage drivers call a "team."

Driving Styles

There are four basic national driving styles: the English, (of which the French and Germans modified and used) Hungarian, Russian, and American Stage-driver. There is a fifth style used in modern combined driving events, which is outlined later in this book.

The English style, which I call the "British Hand," is the one style most universally used in America by the four-in-hand drivers. Some call it the "Coachman Style." With this method, the reins are stacked between the fingers of the left hand and manipulated with the right hand, which also controls the whip. The hands are held perpendicular to the ground. The French method is called the "Full Hand," which is just a variation of the British method. The German or Achenbach method is another variation of the British Hand. It is named after Benno von Achenbach from when he taught at the Hanover Driving School after studying the British coachman style.

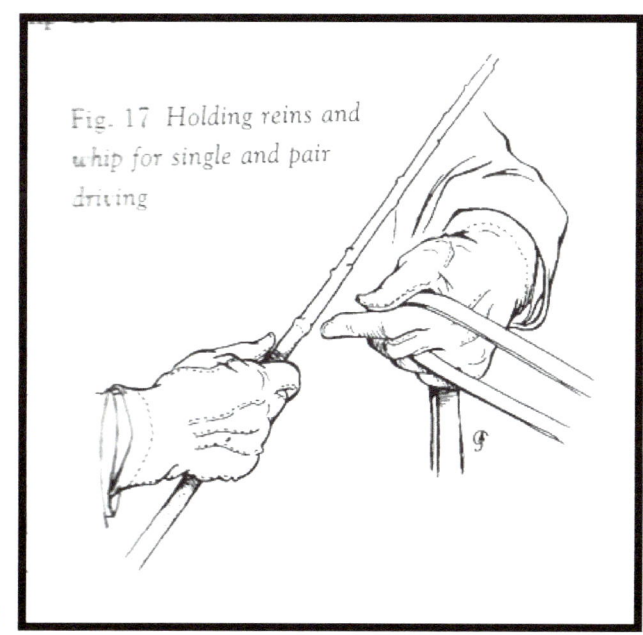

Fig. 17 Holding reins and whip for single and pair driving

The Hungarian method uses a different set of reins and employs a brezel (a hand-grip), which is a handpiece to which the reins are coupled. With this method, the coupling buckle for a pair is close to the driver's hand, which is held in a position parallel to the ground. Traditionally, the Hungarians used double ring snaffle bits on the highly decorated harness.

The Russian Troika is driven with three horses abreast with the middle horse in a full collar with a Duga or shaft bow over its withers. The outside horses canter and wear breast collars. There are four reins in the driver's hand; two from the middle horse and one on the outside of the outside horses. The Vyatka horse was a small horse used in the Troika and the taller, Orlov Trotter, was developed for the aristocrats to reach speeds of 30 miles per hour at the trot with the outside horses cantering.

The American stage-driver holds the two near reins are running up through the left hand separated by the little finger. He feeds the off reins on either side of the middle finger in the right hand. Clubbing the reins is the procedure of placing all reins in the left hand by placing the off reins on top of the hand with the index finger separating the off reins.

Modern drivers also use a system of putting the near reins in the left hand and the off reins in the right with reins clips or buckles. This system is helpful when making turns with speed. Here you see Heather Schneider at the 2015 National Pony driving championship with the two right reins buckled together in the right hand and the two left reins buckled together in the left hand

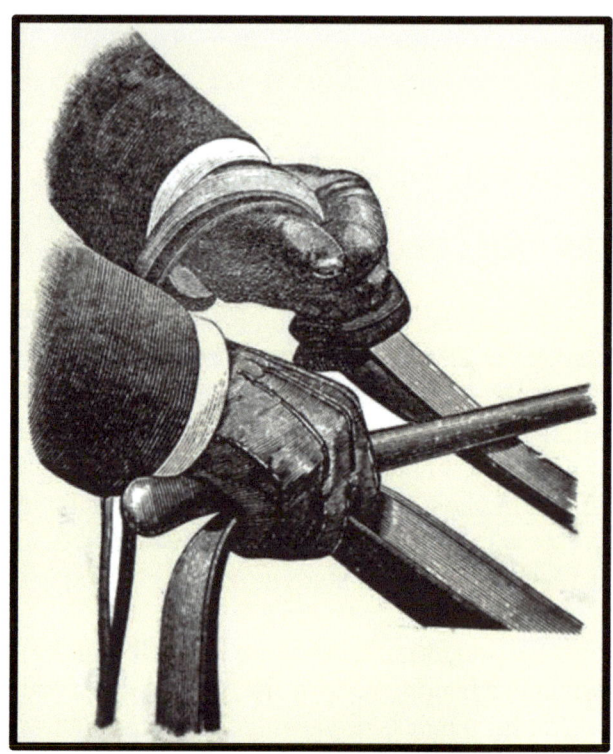

Originally, I held my reins as one would for riding, which is to feed the reins up through the hand and out the top of the clenched fist. Since I rode both in the English and western style, I might transfer the reins to the left hand as I did in western riding to better support the whip in my right. Neck reining is not an option in driving so this maneuver was only used to have freer use of the whip without really understanding techniques.

My first, formal lessons in driving came from the Hungarian Driving Master, Dr. Leslie Kozsely, with a pair of his American Saddlebreds. Therefore, I learned to hold the reins in the left hand with the wrist parallel to the ground.

The British system on the right requires holding the hand be held upright with the knuckles perpendicular, not parallel to the ground with the Hungarian method.

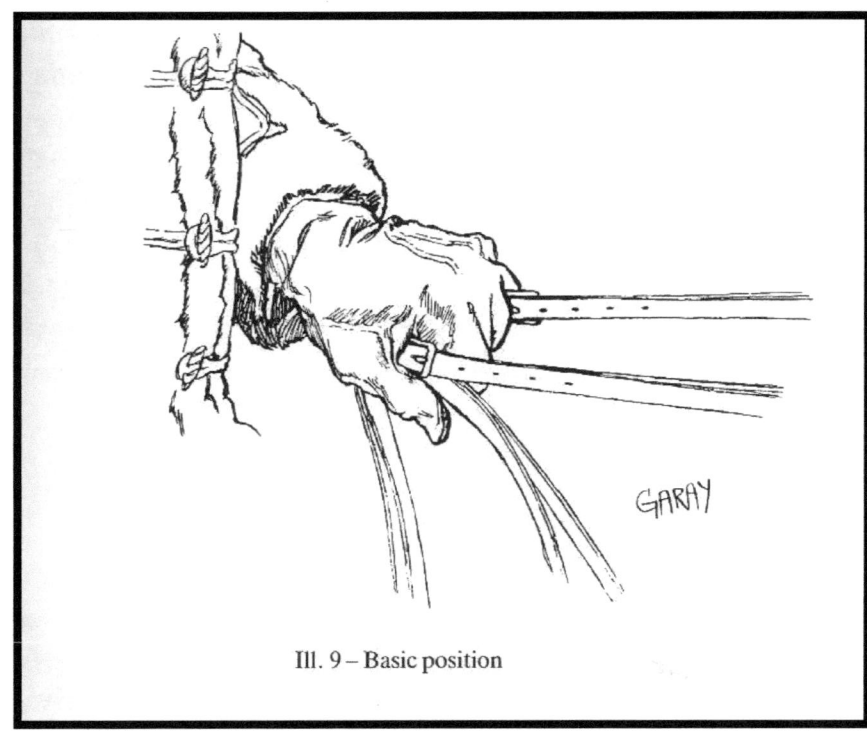

Ill. 9 – Basic position

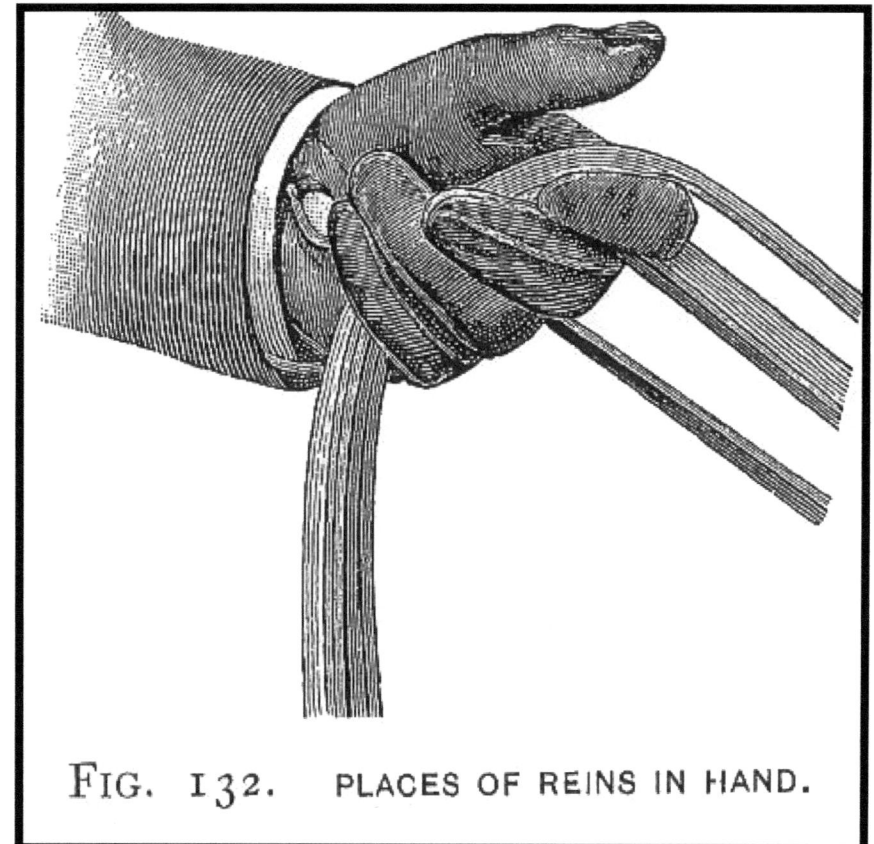

FIG. 132. PLACES OF REINS IN HAND.

The British Hand

The reins are held in the left hand because 90% of us are right-handed. This leaves the more dexterous right hand free to manipulate the reins and use the whip.

In single and pair driving, the near rein is on top of the index, and two fingers separate it from the off rein which is held between the middle finger and the ring finger.

I hold the whip closer to the handle end so as I reach to the near reins of a four; the handle does not get caught in the off reins.

After experiences in the show ring, I discovered the English method was favored by the judges and particularly for the driving of four horses. Luckily George Bowman came to the USA to teach a clinic for friends in South Florida. This was my opportunity to learn something of the British system which was very necessary for driving a four-in-hand.

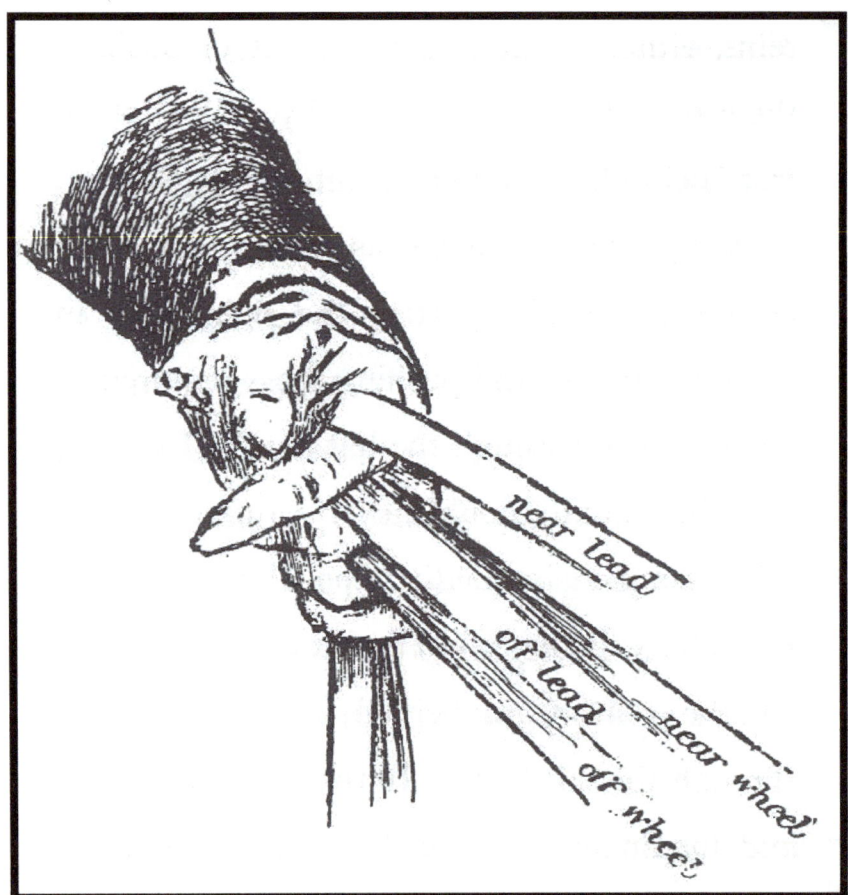

One Hand to Two Hands and the Bridge

Typically, with the British system of driving, the reins are held in the left hand and manipulated with the right hand and the wrist of the left hand. The index finger and the middle finger separate the left and right rein, so there is room for the driver to pass the fingers of the left between the two reins without looking down.

The right hand can them move upward to manipulate the left rein and move downward to manipulate the right rein. The driver can also either move the right hand down to either bridge the reins as you see in the third picture or pick up the right rein without the bridge to move to a two-handed system. The separated two hands are needed for quick turns such as in cones or cross-country work, or in dressage even with a four-in-hand.

The fourth and fifth pictures show how using this method, the two reins can easily be transferred back to the left hand for the classical system which allows the driver the proper use of the whip for signaling the horse and signaling turns and saluting the judge or others along the roadway.

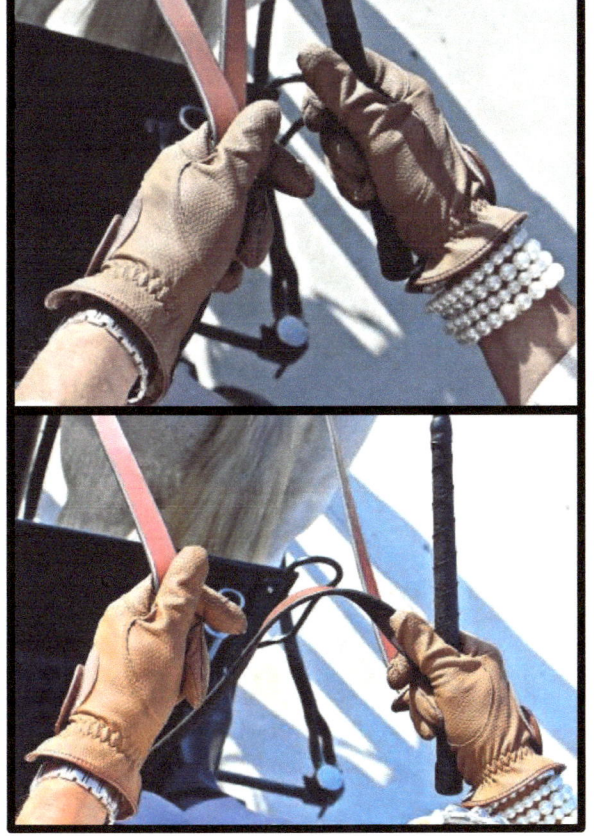
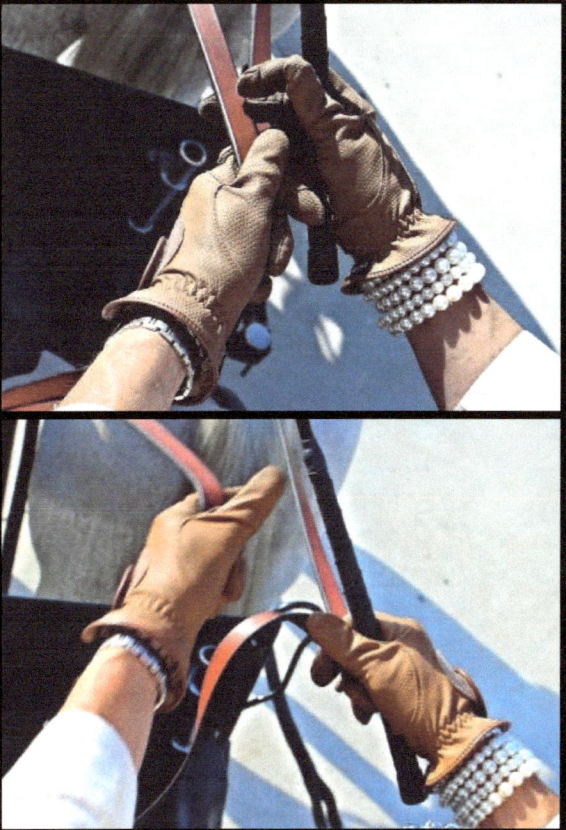
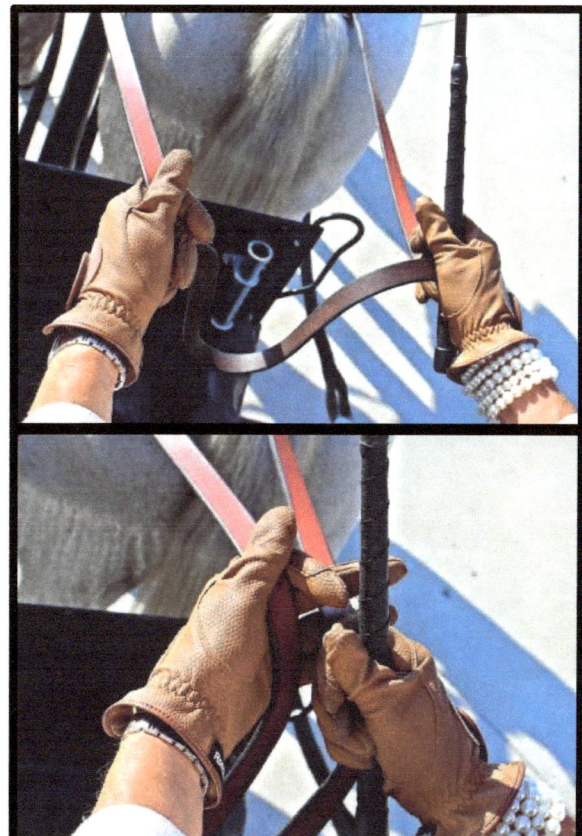

Speak Your Horse's Language

The Whip

At the right are the three basic types of classical whips:

- The Bow Whip (most often used)
- The Drop Thong Whip
- The Buggy Whip

In modern times people have started using telescoping whips to reach the horses in the lead position. It becomes a longer stick with a shorter lash. There is also a short postilion whip for a person who rides the leading, left-hand horse of a pair drawing a coach or carriage.

The stick and lash can be made of differing materials. Classical whips might be made from a Holly tree.

I like to call the whip "the tickle stick." Its basic purpose is to signal the horse to position its body to either gain impulsion or move its hindquarters away from the pressure of the whip.

It can be used on any part of the body as long as you get the desired response, but there are places to tap that seem to get the proper response.

Most often, the whip is used on the inside of the turn at the girth area where a rider's leg would be positioned. It is most often used on the hip on the outside of the turn as an indication for impulsion or speed. It is used on the inside hip to keep the horse from leaning into the turn. It is also used on the outside hip when the driver infrequently asks for the canter.

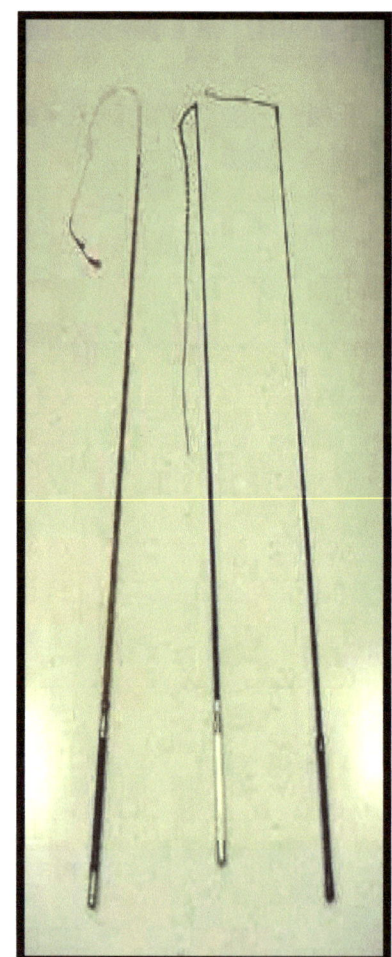

How Long Is the Whip?

The stick and lash may vary in length depending on the type of turnout and the number of horses.

The whip should be long enough to reach the shoulder of the furthest horse from the whip (driver). For instance, in the case of a tandem or four, the whip should reach the shoulder of the lead horse. This sometimes means an 8-foot stick with a 12-foot lash. Whips come in horse size or pony size.

The whip is used on the shoulder to prevent what is called "rubbernecking" or counter bending. The horse should follow his head into the turns. Rubbernecking or counter bending is where the shoulder of the horse leads into the turn. For this purpose, the whip is used on the shoulder that is on the inside of the turn to get the horse to get his attention and turn his head and look in the direction of the turn.

The horse must be sensitized to the whip so that it is neither frightened of its touch nor indifferent to its touch. Most trainers start to sensitize the horse when doing groundwork.

The sensitive horse can become accustomed to the whip through gentle stroking. Some view the whip as an extension of the hand to move the horse away from pressure. Others prefer to view the whip as a replacement for the rider's leg pressure.

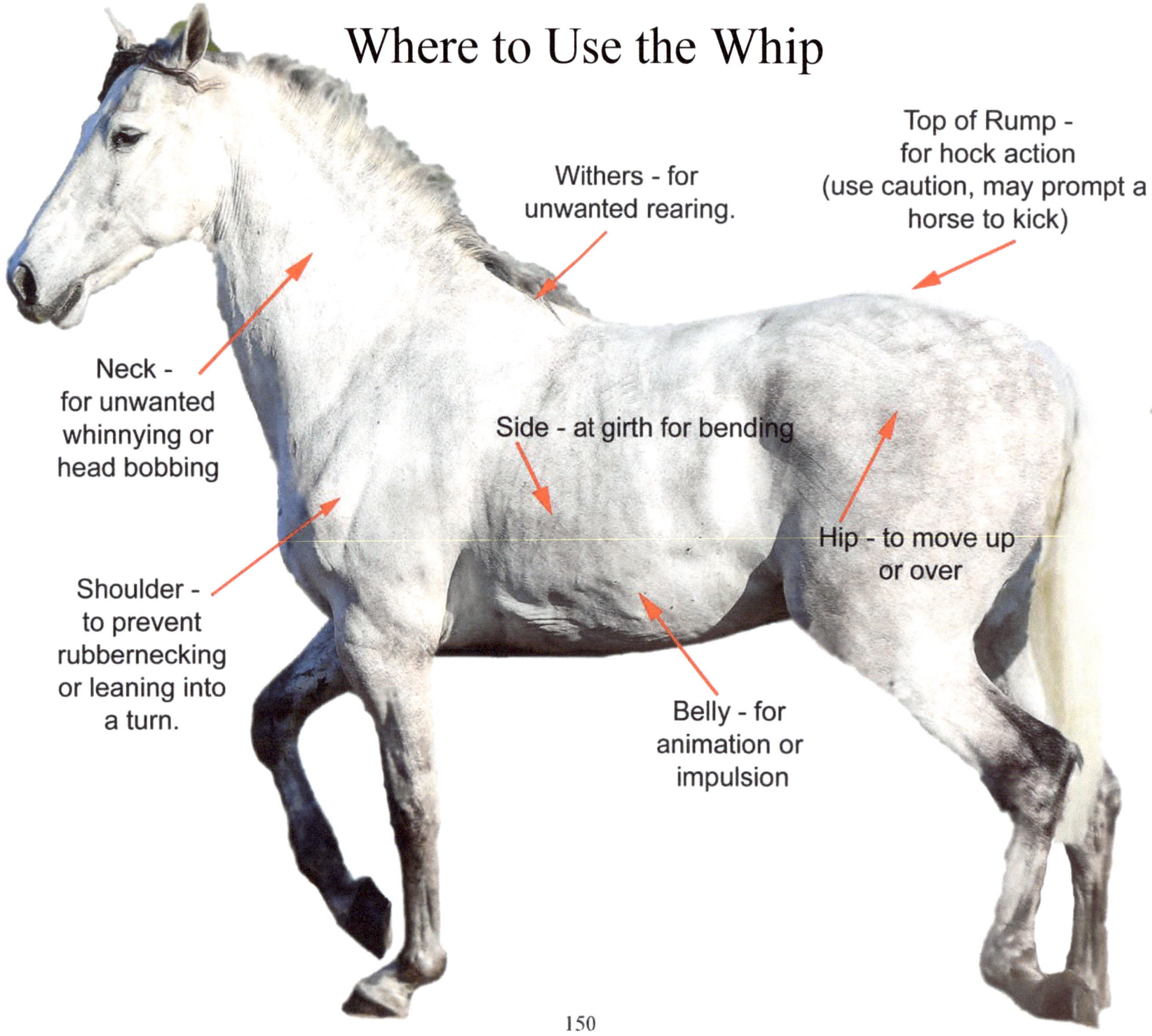

Uses for the Whip

- Move away–like a tickle.
- Punishment–like a slap.
- Caress–like stroking.
- Name recognition–a tap.
- In conjunction with the use of voice: Soothing voice, sharp voice, directive voice.
- To move the horse into the outside rein.
- To create impulsion for proper engagement and balance.

The Harness

There are many books and videos available today on how to harness a single, pair or four-in-hand, so the intent of this book in not to talk about all these things. There are also many clinicians who can help you with harness adjustments, so it is not our intent to talk about this either. Even though, a proper harness, properly adjusted, is a must since the harness and carriage together are integral parts of "talking with tack." Please see our booklet, "Glossary of Harness Parts," by Gloria Austin which is available through www.amazon.com.

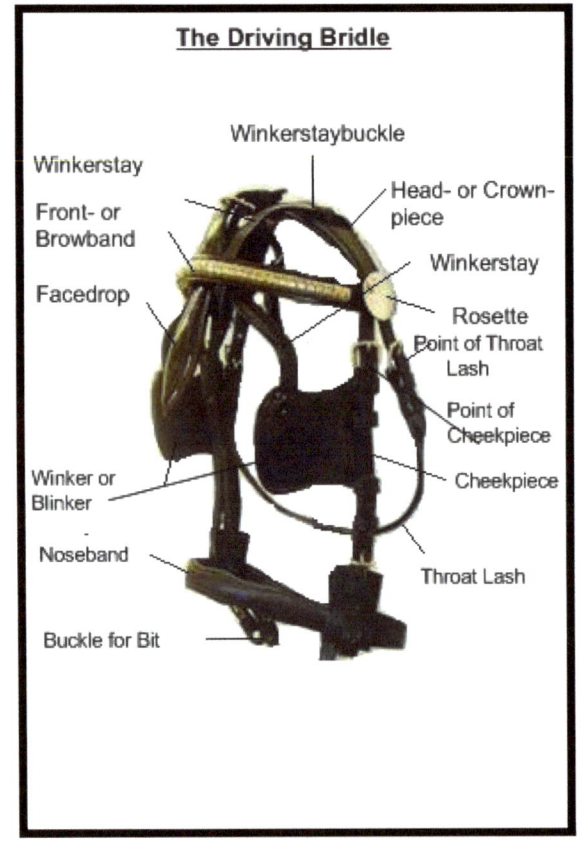

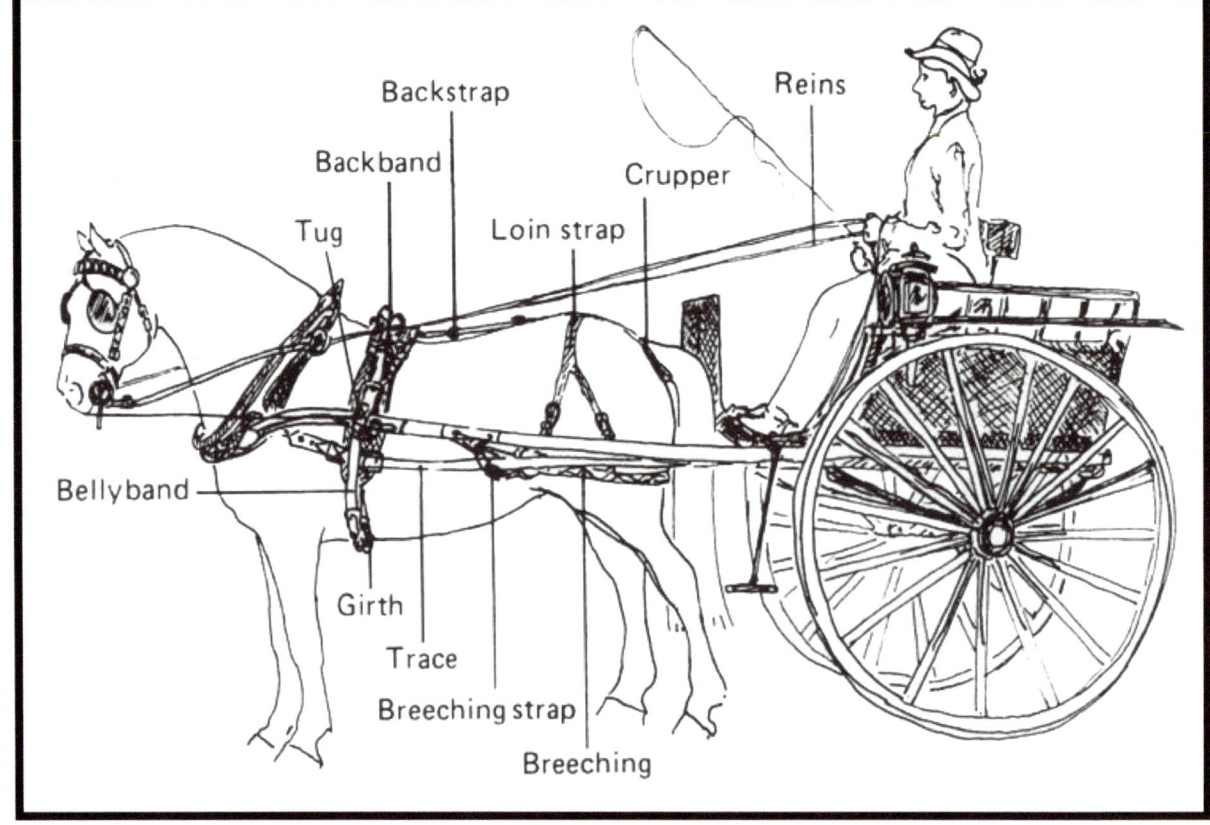

Important Things about Harness

- The horse must be comfortable, which means the harness cannot have rough edges or stitching that pokes the skin. I recommend a quality leather harness made by a respected maker with a good reputation. The harness maker can also help with the proper fit. Always harness and remove the harness in the same sequence.
- The harness must be cleaned after each use. There is no skimping on cleanliness. This means the bits must also be washed. Learn from your harness maker about the right product(s) to use for cleaning your harness. We recommend washing the harness with a cloth dipped into a gallon of water that has one capful of Murphy's Liquid Oil Soap mixed in with it.
- The bridle must fit properly, and the bit must sit properly in the horse's mouth. Always use a gullet strap or other means of ensuring the bridle will not come off. Braiding a string into the mane that is attached to the crown piece of the bridle also works well. The throat latch on a driving bridle is worn tighter than that of a riding bridle also to help prevent the bridle from coming off.
- A full collar is more difficult to fit but allows maximum shoulder extension. It is better for a full collar to be a little too big rather than too small and pinch the neck of the horse.
- Be sure the line of the draft (when the horse is pulling into the collar) is straight and uninterrupted. If the billet on the back band is buckled into the belly band too tight, particularly on a pair, every movement of the horse will pull the back pad downward which interferes with the horse's engagement as it tries to elevate its back in the process of using the core muscles to move its body.
- Breeching, if used, has to ride in the proper position, so it does not ride up under the tail nor ride too low to interfere with the hock action of the horse.
- With a pair, the pole strap and traces have to be adjusted to prevent the horse's hindquarters from hitting the carriage as it holds the carriage back to stop and go downhill.
- When driving a four, it is important not to have the leaders too close to the wheelers to prevent the wheeler from stepping over the lead bars or into the leader's traces.
- Always harness in the same sequence
- Remove the harness in the reverse sequence
- Remember- your horse cannot see his sides in the closed bridle, so do not lead him into things

Choosing the Type of Harness

You must select the right harness for the job. It is a little bit like wearing your tennis clothes to the ball or wearing a western outfit while riding in an English saddle.

Type or Style of Driving

- Fine Harness (often seen in breed showing)
- Pleasure (Traditional)
- Dressage
- Combined Driving
- Marathon and cones
- Racing
- Draft
- Harness Materials
- Leather, nylon, or synthetic.
- White or brass metal.
- Color–black, brown, russet, two-tone.
- Reins–color is always russet, and width depends on the person's hands.
- Buckles, snaps, and quick release
- Things to look for when buying a harness
- Quality leather.
- Stainless steel tongues on the buckles.
- Sound metal fittings.
- Reinforced wear points
- Buy from a reputable harness maker that uses quality materials.

Care of the Harness

Every use:

- Clean thoroughly after each use
- Safety checks: wear and buckles

As needed:

- Dyeing the leather

Driving Horses Wear Blinkers

Blinkers are the rather square or rounded shaped part of the bridle positioned by the eye. They are adjusted, so the horse's eye is centered. We take away much of the horse's peripheral vision to primarily prevent anticipating the use of the whip. The whip is carried by the driver to tap the horse's body as a means of signaling the horse, much as the leg is used in riding.

I call the whip - "the tickle stick." I use the example of coming up behind a person who has not seen your approach, and you suddenly tickle that person on the right side of their rib cage. They should turn their head to the right to see who is doing the tickling. The horse should have the same response: tickle him on the right side near the girth, and he should bend his neck to the right. Tickle him on the left side, and he should bend to the left. The same should be true if the whip is used on the shoulder. Tap on the right shoulder and the horse should look right and tap on the left shoulder, and the horse should bend his neck to the left. The use of the whip on the shoulder is why the whip should be long enough to reach the front shoulder of the horse.

Most driving horses are outfitted with a bridle with blinkers, so we take much of the horse's vision away, meaning we cannot use visual cues to direct the horses. Therefore, the voice and whip are very important in communicating with the driving horse.

Purpose of Blinkers

These blinkers also help to focus the horse's attention on the ground below their feet to avoid any hazards. The driver directs the horse's direction of travel and position of its head, neck, and placement of its feet, but unknown hazards may be under its feet, so it is wise for the horse to see its footing.

Even so, horses involved in modern driving are sometimes outfitted with what is called a "shadow roll." A "shadow roll" blocks the horse's vision underneath its eyes. This is primarily done so these horses move quickly into water or over surfaces that might otherwise scare them and retard their forward momentum and speed through obstacles.

These partial eye coverings also prevent them from seeing scary things approaching from the side or rear. Spooking at such things could cause shying, placing the driver and passengers in peril. We leave these judgments in the hands of the driver.

Removing some of their sights also helps the horse to focus its attention on the driver and our commands given through the reins, voice, and whip.

THE CARRIAGE

This isn't working at all... I should warn others not to put their cart before the horse.

The Carriage

All turnouts, as with all driving, is dictated by the carriage. The carriage must fit the driving one wants to do. Some like to compete in traditional pleasure shows. Others like modern, combined driving that is patterned after three-day eventing. Some participate in breed shows and drive their favorite horse in special driving classes. There are others who like to go to meets and promenade over trails or at steeplechase races. Others prefer to do the recreational driving with friends. Some prefer racing Standardbreds or chariot racing, and in Russia, you might be racing a Troika. No matter what your pleasure, you must pick the correct carriage for the discipline. The carriage dictates the type of harness. The discipline dictates the type or breed of horse.

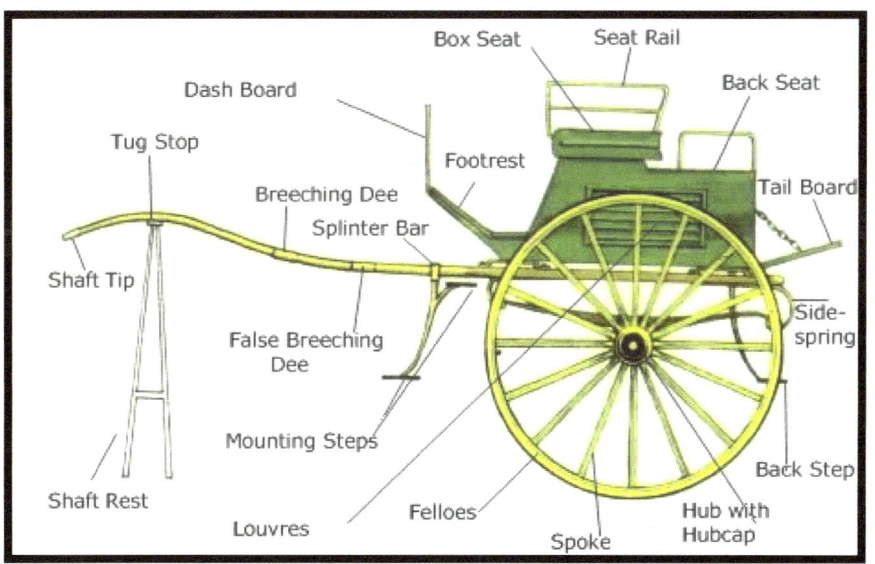

There are two-wheeled carriages and four-wheeled carriages. There are restored antique carriages and new reproductions for use in the recreation of traditional driving. There are modern carriages for presentation and marathon driving at combined driving events. It is important that you attend events to see the type of carriage for the discipline in which you choose to participate. Below you see me driving a large English style coach at a coaching meeting. The gig might be used in a Pleasure Driving Show and the marathon carriage in a Combined Driving Event.

Selection of Carriage

There are many reputable dealers around. I always like to take the personal testimony of those who have a carriage similar to the one I wish to buy. That way I can hear the pros and cons of the particular models.

Auction houses, like Martin's Auctioneers of Pennsylvania, are often where people choose to purchase carriages. Sometimes it is wise to take an experienced amateur driver, a professional driver or a carriage expert with you. I often talk to knowledgeable people at these auctions to learn from their experiences.

Wheels, hubs, single trees, and bolts should always be examined. Shafts or other parts on antique carriages are sometimes cracked but covered with filler and paint. This makes it difficult to know the soundness of a vehicle.

Your seating requirements may dictate the model of carriage you buy. The primary driving force in carriage selection is the driving you desire and the soundness of the carriage.

Type of Carriage

Your driving dictates the type of carriage.

Your carriage must fit the size, height, and style of your horse.

- Carriage choices include:
    - Two-wheeled
        - Antique in need of restoration
        - Restored antique
        - Newly built reproduction
        - Modern
    - Four-Wheeled
        - Antique in need of restoration
        - Restored antique
        - Newly built reproduction
        - Modern

Two or Four Wheels?

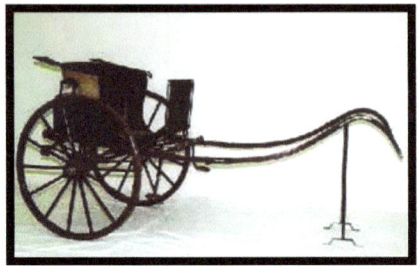

    Again, the discipline you choose may dictate either a two-wheeled or four-wheeled carriages. Also, the training level of your horse can influence your choice.

    I recommend you that you do not move to a four-wheeled carriage until your horse can stand quietly and only back the number of steps you command. Backing in harness is one of the last things for which we train since backing when not commanded can jackknife a four-wheeled carriage and tip it over. Once your horse is trained, a four-wheeled carriage can be more comfortable and safer when moving fast through cones or across country-course.

    Some pleasure shows offer gig classes or Long Island cart classes. These vehicles are two-wheeled so that everyone will be in carriages of these types.

    There are also classes exclusively for runabouts or bonneted phaetons. Again, I encourage you to purchase "The Gloria Austin Carriage Collection" book to learn about the various types of traditional carriages.

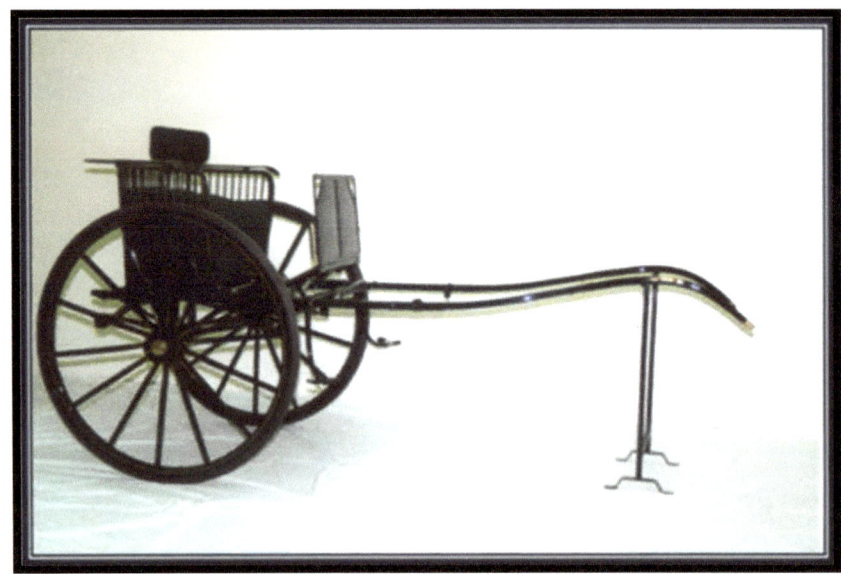

The Antique Carriage

These carriages have to be examined carefully when purchasing, but, once restored properly for driving, are far more comfortable than newly made carriages.

When purchasing, you must check for cracks and loose spokes. Beware - new paint may cover defects.

Check single trees, roller bolts, and shaft attachments before purchasing and before and after use.

Sometimes wheels and axles of one carriage are changed out and put with the other-than-the-original body. Get an experienced person to help you with your selection and get tips on how to look for these problems.

The Newly Manufactured Carriage

Make sure you have interviewed persons who own the carriage you are considering There are top manufacturers here in the US and there are many European manufacturers who have US dealers.

Care of the Carriage

Whether you have a new or antique carriage, regular maintenance is required.

A good carriage jack(right) is a wise investment. It is necessary for working on wheels and also comes in handy when cleaning.

Brakes may need servicing and new fluid if hydraulically activated. Scrub brakes (right) may need new plates.

Whether it is a coach or a lightweight training cart, the wheel and axles have to be maintained. Antique carriages require greasing of the axle stub and checking of the leather washers (left) for wear and replacing if worn to ensure a good snug fit.

Some larger hubs (usually on heavier more formal vehicles) may have an oil reservoir in the hub that should be monitored with each use to ensure proper lubrication. Most modern carriages have roller bearings which may be greased periodically much the same as automobile wheels are today. Wheels should be checked for tight fitment of the spokes. A well-trained wheelwright can tighten a loose wheel. Generally, as the wheel rotates, the spoke pointing at the ground should do so at a 90° angle to the ground.

Cleaning before and after every use is not only essential to keep the carriage looking nice, but also a good opportunity to take a glance at all the parts to check for the security of the bolts and nuts, check for blemishes, the condition of leather, etc.

Places to Train

Driving Locations

We most likely will not be taking our horse to the local coffee shop waiting for the barista to give him a lump of sugar but we will be driving in many locations and environments. Whether driving at a show, training at home, or out for a pleasure drive, we will encounter many environments, obstacles, and situations. It is important to be prepared for the many places we might be driving our horse.

Round Pen

The Round Pen is a great place for groundwork. It provides us the ability to:

- Work in a controlled area.
- Give the horse firmly, basic training.

Arena or Dressage Ring

An arena or driven dressage ring (40m x 80m for small size or 40m x 100m for large size) are safe places to practice driving. These locations provide the opportunity to:

- Practice the uses of the aids.
- Practice various gaits.
- Practice maneuvers: turns, halt, rein back.

Roadway and Animal Training

Because so much of our driving is done on the roadway, it is necessary for driving horses to be accustomed to traffic. Again, progressive steps can be taken to help the horse overcome its fear of the vision and noise of automobiles, trucks, buses, and farm equipment.

It is great if you can pasture beside the road or lead or ride the horse in traffic first. Then the trainer might want to ground drive beside a road with a header to accustom the horse to the world of roadway and traffic.

Those with an experienced driving horse can acquaint the new driving horse to traffic by hitching it beside an experienced, probably older horse.

Sometimes we forget that our suburban or even rural trained horses are not acquainted with farm animals so that the same procedure can be used here. My driving horses Curley and Shadow went to a cattle ranch to do ranch work under saddle so they would not be afraid of cows. It is best if horses can be exposed to the sights and sounds of smaller animals like goats and pigs, too.

Slow moving vehicle signs that meet Federal regulations are a necessity when driving on public roadways. Places like "Driving Essentials" sell ones that easily attach to your carriage. Try to keep the sign 3 to 6' from the road surface.

Training the horse to traffic is sometimes a challenge for some horses. If you have a pasture with secure fencing near a roadway, a horse pastured there can become accustomed to traffic on its own.

If possible gradually introduced the horse to traffic in a non-threatening way by first leading near a highway, then ground driving near traffic, and then hook up to a carriage and do the same. The horse has to become familiar to traffic from the front and also from the rear.

Driving on a highway always poses some danger just as driving a car on public roads. Investigating the rule-of-the-roads in your state before driving is a wise decision. In some states, horses have the right of way.

In general, horse-drawn carriage drivers have to observe the all the regulations that apply to regular traffic–such as stopping at stop signs and lights that indicate such. All carriage drivers should learn hand signals for the passenger and the driver. Carriage Association of American's proficiency testing requires this.

I do not recommend waving traffic to pass from the carriage because of the eagerness of our litigious society. If problems occur, you may be brought to blame.

The Right Side of the Road

Why do postilion riders ride the near horse? Why do we sit on the right side of the carriage? Why do we drive on the ride side of the road? Why do classical forms of reinsmanship place the reins in the left hand? What carriage in history had the drivers sitting in the center of the front seat? Who developed the marathon carriage where navigators ride standing in the back?

Every carriage driver should know the answers to these questions if they are to be involved with an age-old means of transportation–the horse and carriage. The simple answer is that most people are right-handed. More than 90% of our population throughout history has been right-handed. The explanation is far more complex if one examines the history of driving horses.

Postilion driving rides the near horse so he might hold the whip for directing the off-horse in his more dexterous right hand. Also, there was a history of officers carrying a long blade in a scabbard on their left hip, so the right hand could easily access the weapon.

Sitting on the right side of the carriage came from the time of early civilizations where the charioteer stood on the right side of the carriage so he might wield a weapon to protect the right flank while the Bowman protected the left.

Driving on the right side of the road in America has been in existence since Colonial times when ox-teams, horseback riders, and horses pulled cargo wagons. The wagons were driven with a jerk-line from a teamster walking beside horses or oxen. Sometimes the teamster sat on a "lazy board" attached to the left side of the wagon box.

Classical forms of driving evolved from the same principle of right-handedness. If the reins are carried in the left hand, the right hand is free to manipulate the reins, wield the whip, or signal and operate the brake lever or brake wheel. The British Hand was studied at great length by Achenbach who promulgated the system for use by the German military.

The coachmen who drove full-state carriages sat in the middle of a seat covered by a hammer-cloth. Modern combined driving drivers have taken to sitting in the center of the front box seat.

Always Use Studs or Borium

Carriage driving horses are regularly in situations where they need traction for pulling or holding back a load. The carriage, and specifically coaches, are driven on hard surfaces where falling can be particularly hazardous. There are several options to give traction to horseshoes - borium, drill-tech or drive- in or screw-in studs.

Borium or Drill-Tech is a combination of filler material, usually brass, and very hard metal (drill tech is made of crushed up metal drills) that when heated along with the shoe, permanently bonds. Another option to add traction to a shoe is to use drive-in studs. To do this, the farrier will use a drill press to create additional holes in the horseshoe and then drive the slightly flared plugs of hardened metal into the shoe.

Some drivers prefer screw-in studs, but these require considerable work to use. The challenge is to prevent the horse from slipping on hard surfaces and in grass or mud. These traction systems have to be used but in the process, they "stick" to the road surface and can pull the shoe from the horse's foot. Therefore toe clips are necessary. I find toe clips work better on front shoes and side clips better behind. Side clips offer more support when the horses shift its weight to the rear or in turn.

(Some information is from the American Farrier's Journal.)

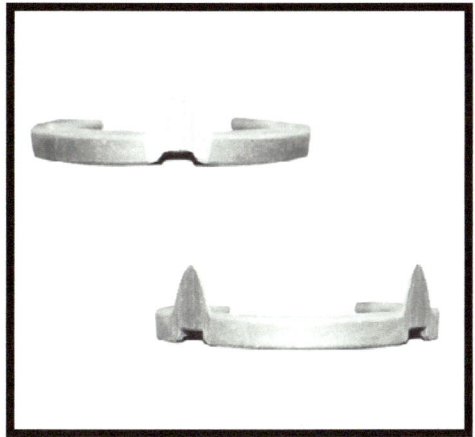

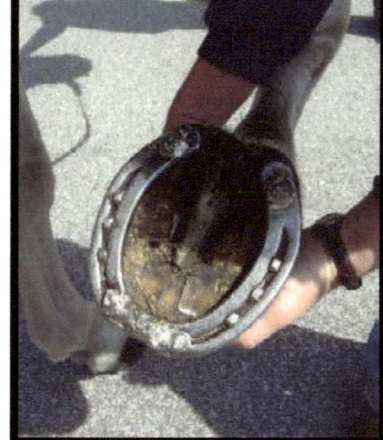

Water Crossing

All the horse training requires a slow, methodical progression of steps. A horse can be walked to "sniff" the water, step in the water, walk in the water, and then be ridden through the water. After put to, the carriage the horse should be walked and trotted through the water crossing. These incremental exposures will produce gains. The goal is to get your horse to walk, stop, and trot or even canter through water and around obstacles.

Bridge

Bridges and other changes of the surface can be approached with the same slow, methodical progression of steps. When starting, let the horse sniff or even paw at the surface at first. He or she is just testing to see if it is safe. "Nagging'" works just as it does for loading a horse in a trailer. It is a matter of getting the horse is accustomed to stepping on differing surfaces. Because horses don't like changes in light and dark, a covered bridge many require encouragement on the part of the rider or driver.

I prefer starting a horse over a faux bridge like the one pictured on the left. I also do like bridges that have guarded approaches, so the horse is directed over the bridge's platform. The sounds of each bridge can be very different, as in the case of this covered bridge where sound resonating off the covered section is different from the platform without a cover. Once the horse has experiences moving over differing surfaces, it begins to trust your judgment about crossing a scary surface; it becomes easier to cross all types of surfaces.

I still always look and focus through to beyond the obstacle and always give a voice command to keep the cadence over the upcoming surface.

Driving Away from the Barn

Special precautions need to be taken when going out for a drive that is away from the barn.

You should
- Let someone know where you plan to go and how long you might be gone.
- Take a companion with you.
- Take a cell phone with you.
- Be sure to have a spares kit and a Leatherman.

Learn Your Traffic Signals and Salutes

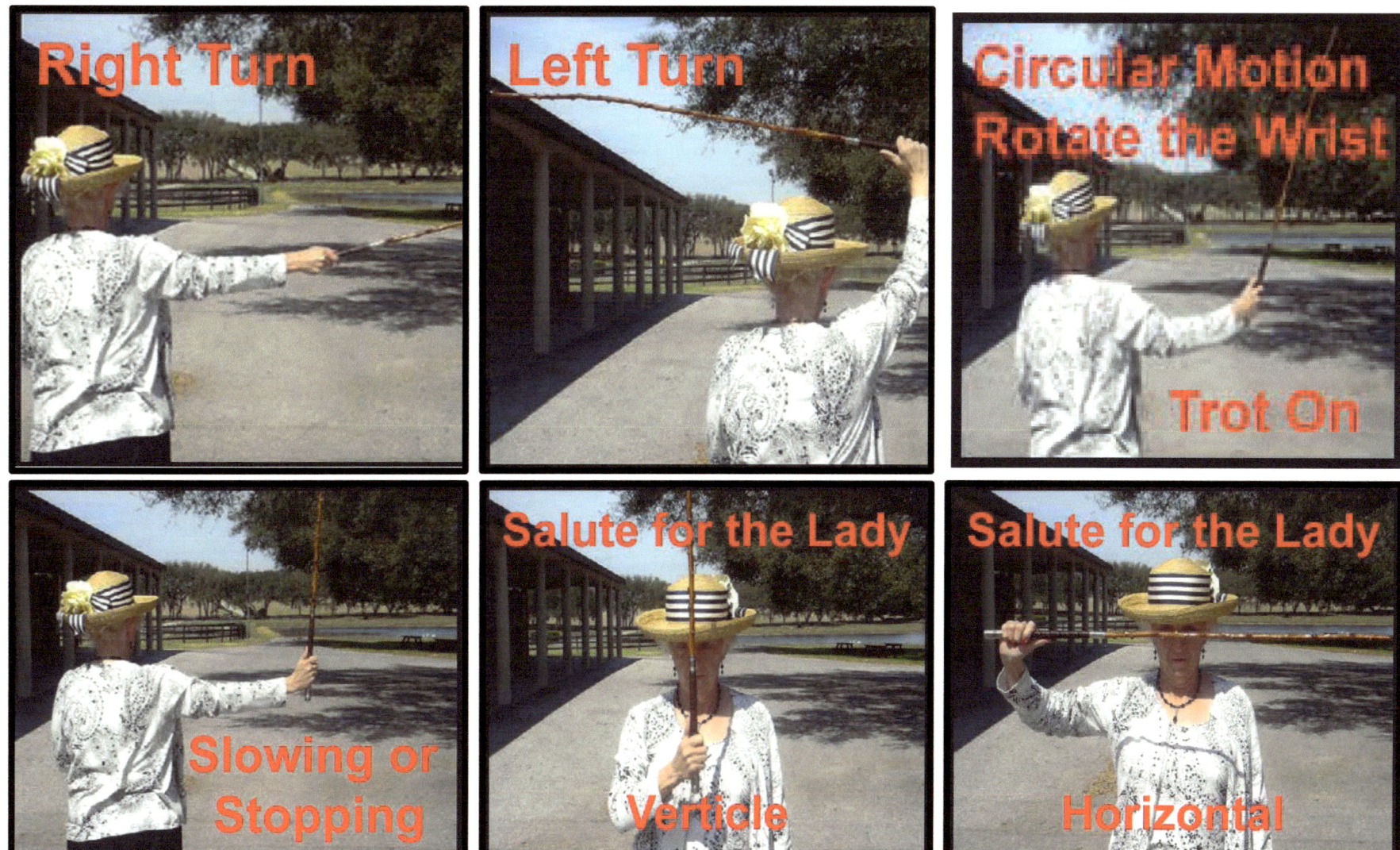

Note
    Salute for the Gentleman: The Whip is placed in the left hand, on top of the reins. The hat is removed with the right hand, and the arm is extended off to the right with the hat in the same position it should appear when on the drivers head. The driver then nods his head and replaces his hat and takes up his whip in the right hand

SAFETY

Most Common Problems

One of the most common problems we see with drivers is that the driver is over horsed. This means that the horse is too spirited or too forward moving or too quick or too overfed for the driver. Less experienced people should start with a well-trained older horse that is not overly eager to move into his or her task. It is OK to ask the horse twice to do something if you are less than skilled yourself. We all like talented, pretty horses, but sometimes it is best to start or advance with a horse that is suited to our level of driving. Some horses adapt readily to the skill level of a new driver, but with the visibility of a strong, aggressive horse in competition, the driver is always tempted to buy more horse than needed for the job or level of the driver's ability. It is best to start with a nice quiet horse and move to a more athletic or spirited horse as our skill level advances.

The second most common problem carriage drivers have is working with a staff that does not know horses, have not bonded with your horses, don't know what to do to prevent accidents, don't know their jobs, and don't know what to do when things go wrong. The key is to have a well-trained staff that knows your horses and you. They should know what to do and when to do it. It takes good observant people to keep a driver, passengers and the horses safe.

Equipment breakage and improper adjustment of equipment is another common problem. Continued inspection of equipment is necessary for safe driving.

Improper bitting of the driving horse can also be a problem. Driving horses should be driven in driving bits, most often a curb bit.

What is Safety?

- 🐎 Safety is a well-trained horse.
- 🐎 Safety is a well-trained and alert driver.
- 🐎 Safety has assistants or grooms that know what to do to prevent a problem and what to do in the event of an emergency.
- 🐎 Safety is a sound carriage that is properly constructed and maintained.
- 🐎 Safety is a properly fitted, adjusted and maintained harness.
- 🐎 The role of grooms on the ground is to make sure the bridle does not come off the horse when at a halt. They can also aid in keeping the horse's head in position and still at the halt. They also should monitor the traffic at intersections with a four-in-hand since the driver sits some 21 feet back from the intersection.
- 🐎 All people involved with the horse should know the three basic rules of safety.
- 🐎 The driver should always carry the whip. You never know when something might frighten the horse, and without the use of your legs as a rider, it is the only way to get the horse to go forward and not back up and jackknife the carriage.

To Be Safe, You Need

- **A well-trained driver that knows**
    - The body language of the horse.
    - That communication is built on bonding and trust.
    - The aids for driving.
    - The temperament of the horse.
    - The use of imaging and positive thoughts.

- **A well-trained horse that**
    - Is balanced and impulsed.
    - Understands the cues.
    - Can keep an even cadence.
    - Can halt and stand quietly.
    - Can bend and move straight and laterally.

- **A sound carriage that is**
    - In good repair.
    - Serviced regularly.
    - Sturdy.
    - Of the proper design and size for discipline and horse.

- **A strong, effective harness**
    - Suited for the job.
    - Comfortable on the horse.
    - With a bit that is proper for signaling and control.

To be Safe, You Need Skilled Assistants

Well skilled assistants
- Are familiar with the horse and can at least ride.
- Understand leading and loading
- Understand the use of voice
- Understand the principles of applying for pressure and release
- Understand the horse's lack of peripheral vision
- Know the terms associated with the harness and carriage
- Know their role:
  - Head the horses and keep the head in position side to side and up and down
  - Keep the bridle on when to a halt
  - Have a calming demeanor and know deep breathing techniques
  - Know techniques of calming the horse
  - Know how and when to "giggle" the bit
  - Know how and when to scratch the withers
  - Know about hanging on the neck
- Have driving skills if possible
- Know traffic directions
  - Dismounting and mounting on the move
  - Intersection monitoring
  - Warning of potential hazards–passing, animals running up on either side
- Understand emergency procedures
  - Getting to the horse's head
  - Trace down, leg over trace, hames off the collar, bits caught, broken harness or carriage parts
- Know care and management of the horses, harness, and carriage
- have licensing and skill at driving the truck and a large trailer

What Are the Three Basic Safety Rules?

1) Never remove the bridle while the horses are put to the carriage.

2) Never leave the horse unattended when put to the carriage.

3) 'First in Last Out'–No passengers on the carriage without the driver in position.

Problems

Despite knowing and practicing all safety precautions, problems can occur. It is important that the driver and all assistants know what to do when problems happen. Some potential problems include:

Out of control

Broken harness

Broken carriage

Dropped rein

Tail over rein

Horse falls

Horse kicks over trace

Horse rears over the pole or shafts

Pole breaks

Out of Control Horse

Stay calm and use a soft voice to sooth the horse. Use a calming voice and say "Steady" "Easy" or "Whoa."

It is important to react within 3 seconds, preferably sooner. Take hold of the horse's mouth through the reins and bit but don't freeze on the reins. A sawing motion, or back-and-forth movement of the bit, may work. Use hands, arms, and legs to come to a semi-stand to apply pressure to the mouth of the horse. Sometimes you may have even to release pressure and reapply pressure through the reins.

Turn the horse in a circle if space allows. A large circle at first and make it smaller and smaller but not so tight as to tip the carriage.

Another option is to move into rough terrains like heavy grass or a plowed field or deep footings like sand or snow.

I believe that training of a horse to return to a rhythmic pace when frightened is important.

Broken Equipment or Tip Over

It is always advisable to work with an assistant who can get to the horse's head as soon as possible. If something breaks, halt. Sometimes the driver becomes so frightened he or she forgets to say the word "whoa." Now is the time to say whoa and stay calm.

With the assistant at the horse's head, ask the passengers to dismount and then the driver may get off the carriage if circumstances seem to warrant. The driver should still control the horse(s) with the reins after all are dismounted, and the horse is disconnected from the carriage.

Use the brake if the carriage is fitted with one and have a knowledgeable assistant that can control the horse if necessary.

Unhitch the horse before making repairs.

Use spares (tools) and make necessary repairs before hitching, reloading, and proceeding.

If repairs are not possible on site, you will have to lead horses to a safe location until returning to your home stable. Part of your spares carried onboard the carriages are halters and leads - one for each horse driven. Be sure you use a safe procedure when exchanging a halter for a bridle. (The bridle should never be removed when the horse is attached to the carriage.) If you choose to lead your horse to a safe destination using the bridles, make sure both reins are attached to the bit or in the case of a pair, attach the coupling rein to the inside of each horse's bit so that each bit has two reins attached.

What if a Horse Falls?

Calmness is a great virtue.

Horses try to get to their feet in a hurry so sometimes they stumble and quickly recover.

If a horse falls and is completely down when hitched to a carriage, an assistant should get to the horse's head as quickly as possible, approaching the horse from the top of its head, not near its legs which might flail in an attempt to get upright. Hold the horse's head to the ground until the harness is disconnected from the carriage and the carriage is removed and pulled well back from the horse. Only then ask the horse to stand, keeping free of its legs.

A horse cannot stand without the use of his head. (Remember the earlier diagram? 90% of the balance in head and neck.). So as long as the head is pinned to the ground that horse cannot stand.

Often you can re-hitch and proceed if the horse is not injured and equipment not broken.

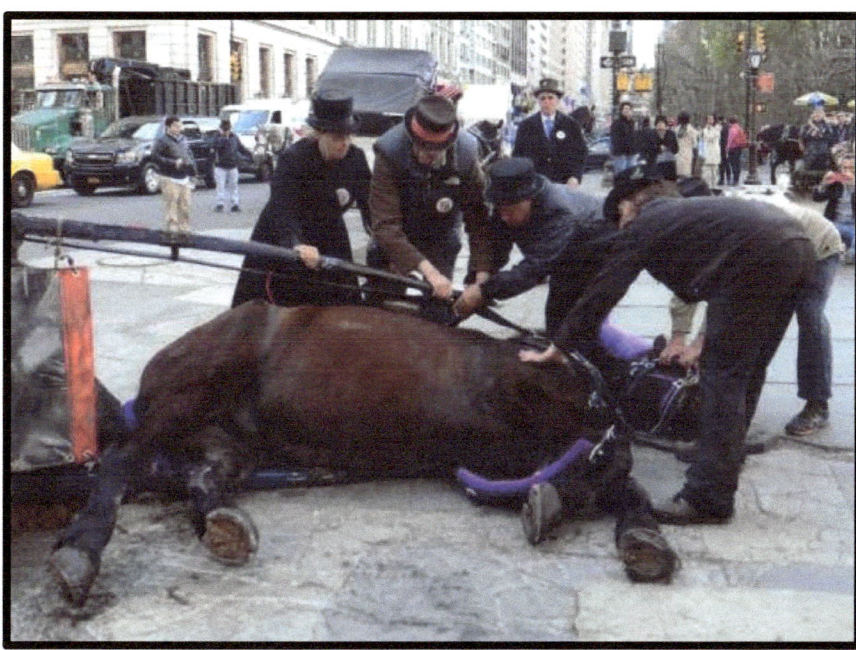
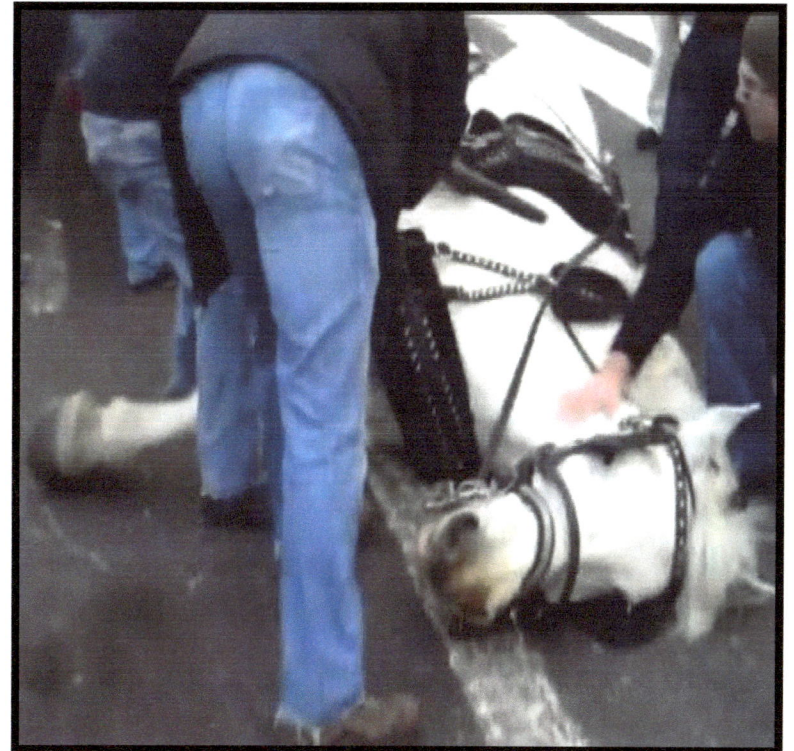

The Three Second Rule

You have three seconds to get the attention of a reactive frightened horse.

Some horses just stop and freeze in place when frightened, others react by running, shying or bolting.

With the horse that stops, sometimes it is best to let the horse collect their thoughts about a response and then gently encourage the horse to move forward. Forward is always good if you have assessed the potential danger and warrant that moving forward is the best plan.

The bit is the most effective way to get the unthinking horse not to take flight. The sensitivity of the mouth and lips can work in your favor to get the horse to maintain its attention on its work and your directive. Quickly get contact with the horse's mouth with the reins and bit. Sometimes a seesawing motion of the bit will help. You have to get its attention as quickly as possible.

Establishing a cadence when you train a horse helps. Then if the horse scurries for a bit, it will realize the safe thing is to keep its normal cadence.

Using effective, consistent, communication to build trust will help in these situations.

Again, there are no hard and fast rules, but try to get the horse's attention back on you and its work as quickly as possible.

Truck and Trailer Safety

Many times, we will be driving to a location away from home with our horses and carriages. Our horses will need to learn to load in a trailer, and we need to keep them safe in the trailer.

- Train your horse to load–"Leading and Loading" by John Lyons is a good read.
- Don't get caught inside the trailer when loading the horse
- Have quick release ties for the horses
- Be sure the trailer has butt bars and tailgates - and use them
- Clean and remove mats and inspect the floor after each use.
- Check for wasps in the trailer before loading horses.
- Keeping the trailer clean gives us the opportunity to make a safety check on the trailer. Large truck stops often have washing bays for our trucks and trailers. Also be sure to pressure wash trailer interiors.
- Service truck and trailer periodically
- Every trip: check lights, brakes, and tires
- Tires over six to seven years old should be replaced.
- Carry flare, tools and emergency equipment
- Pay strict attention to cargo trailers as well.
-

Driving the Truck and Trailer
Keeping horses comfortable while driving is important too.

- Make wide turns
- Use your mirrors
- Practice backing up
- Set your brake control
- Test your trailer's brakes and lights before every trip
- Always be sure to allow for a safe stopping distance.

Remember When Driving Your Horse

YOU MUST

- Know how to read a horse's body language
- Understand the balance of the horse
- Know how impulsion is created
- Know what a driving bit is
- Know how the bit is effectively used
- Know how the whip is used
- Know how the voice used
- Know your mind and emotions and how they affect your horse
- Be aware of what motivates your interest in the horse and of the good brain chemicals that connect you and your horse.
- Understand how to bond and develop trust in the relationship
- Use positive role models
- Act and dress like a winner
- Act confident and enjoy the experience
- Learn to cope with stress
- Set a plan with goals
- Work toward unconscious competence
- Drive with your head
- Use the aids
- Remember the rules
- Have fun

YOUR HORSE MUST

- Yield to the bit
- React to the whip
- Respond to your voice

Role Models

We usually think about role models for children or youth, but adults who want to be successful also need role models when starting a new activity or becoming better at an activity like carriage driving.

You may already know a successful carriage driver that you admire but have not studied and tried to emulate. A role model should be someone with similar skills and assets to yourself, but a bit further along in their driving. Recognize that this is a "guide" for you and not someone you have to follow exactly. One good way to prevent this from being a problem is to have multiple role models. Sometimes these role models can become your mentor or teachers and personally help you with your development of skills. Sometimes role models can be your rivals in the show ring.

Early in my driving experience, my role model was a woman by the name of Holly Momberger. She was always winning blue ribbons with her single horse put to a runabout at Walnut Hill Farm Driving Competition. I watched her. I saw how she warmed up. I saw how she dressed, how she sat in her carriage. I watched how her horse moved. I watched how she handled the reins and whip. She inspired me to want to be like her and to win just like she did.

I also observed and listened to her when she came out of the show ring, and she was always talking about what she could have done better. This told me that she always wanted to improve even though she had won the top prize. She was always striving to improve her performance. She was always passionate about what she was doing. And she was persistent and kept showing up at competitions. Darn! I was in her division driving a single Saddlebred when she drove her experienced elderly Morgan. This told me I had to hang in there and give my Saddlebred lots of experiences and keep showing up myself.

When it came to driving four horses, my role model was Jack Pemberton. He was driving four to a large coach at the Royal Winter Fair in Toronto, Canada. Sometimes you have to find role models that are not of your same sex. At the time I knew of no women four-in-hand drivers. Jack looked so proud sitting atop his huge coach, dressed "to the nines" and chatting with his guests who were also bedecked with their finest clothes. I thought, if an elderly gentleman like him can to that, I surely could.

As I explained when interviewed as a Living Legend in Lake County, Florida and asked about my greatest accomplishments: I responded - "being a role model for others." Thanks, Holly and Jack. I passed it on.

Act and Dress like a Winner

Often acting like a winner and dressing like a winner makes a difference. Skill development is only part of the game. The positive aspects of looking good are amazing.

Sitting upright with confidence and dressing well can reflect on your attitude and the impression you give to others. As we discussed earlier core muscle development contributes to your upper body frame which is a key to rein handling and looking competent. With a proper frame and looking in the direction of the turn, the horse can more easily understand your aids.

You can take your cues for a dress from others that are successful in driving, or you can learn from images of winners in the type of competition in which you are participating. If you act confident and enjoy the experience, you are halfway there. Smiling and those lines around your eyes that come from smiling can release chemicals in your brain that make you feel better and project an air of confidence.

In 1977, I read *The Women's Dress For Success Book* by John T. Molloy about the effect of clothing on a person's success in business and personal life. The book was not just an opinion but based on scientific research. Well, I found the research to be true in most life experiences.

Successful Driving Requires

- Knowledge of horses: Understanding how to communicate with a horse is important to be successful and most of all, safe.

- Personal understanding: It is important to set achievable goals and to know what you don't know to get help along the way.

- Observation skills: You need to be able to read your horse in any situation and react appropriately.

- Patience: Working with horses can be like working with children; you need to be kind and patient to help the horse learn and respond properly.

- Skill development: There is much to learn at every stage from driving singles to multiples. Get help along the way and enjoy the process.

- Consistency: Horses learn by repetition, so it is important to be consistent with your training methods.

- Focus: Have a goal and stay focused on achieving that goal before moving on.

- Attention: Things can happen quickly when working with horses so pay attention and stay on task.

- Understanding: Learn to understand all aspects of carriage driving so that you and your horse can have a good time and be safe.

- Repetition, Repetition, Repetition: The more you work together with your horse, the more you will both achieve.

- Practice, Practice, Practice: Practice really does make perfect and also provides a wonderful opportunity for you to bond with your horse.

- Skilled assistants: Assistants need to be knowledgeable about carriage driving and have a good understanding of working with horses.

Educate Yourself

- 🐎 I encourage new drivers to attend competitions as a spectator and also attend conferences and clinics.
- 🐎 Talk to competitors and observe the good ones.
- 🐎 Attend local club functions and participate as much as you can.
- 🐎 Take lessons from competent recognized trainers and professionals.
- 🐎 Join driving organizations and read their publications. "The Carriage Journal," published by the Carriage Association of America, "The Whip," published by The American Driving Society and "The Driving Digest," published by Ann L. Pringle, are all good magazines.
- 🐎 Watch instructional videos from recognized leaders in the discipline in which you are interested. YouTube also has many good videos. Make sure you look at ones within your driving discipline.
- 🐎 Purchase and read books even if they are not by contemporary authors. Many of the old books offer good advice on horses and driving.
- 🐎 Many of the natural horsemanship trainers offer insights into reading the behavior of the horse. Be sure you drive with a proper driving bridle and a driving bit.

Speak Your Horse's Language

CAA Driver Proficiency Program

Participation in this program will help to increase your awareness and knowledge of driving, how to do so safely and correctly, and earn you a CAA Driver Proficiency Certificate.

In addition to evaluating drivers' proficiency at the various levels, this program also allows for those interested in becoming driving instructors to accomplish the prerequisites at the levels. This will ensure the standard for traditional driving and horsemanship skills will continue.

- Instructors
  Evaluators
  Level 1
  Level 2
  Level 3

For more information contact:

The Carriage Association of America
3915 Jay Trump Road
Lexington, KY 40511

859-231-0971,
859-231-0973 (fax)

info@caaonline.com,
www.caaonline.com

enjoyment for all...

challenging and fun for the young driver...

beautiful to watch and exhilarating to do.....

daring....

Speak Your Horse's Language

about friendships!

www.ingramcontent.com/pod-product-compliance
Lightning Source LLC
Chambersburg PA
CBHW041152070526

44584CB00004B/285